SIZZLING BARBECUE RECIPES

UK COOKERY EDITOR
Katie Swallow

EDITORIAL
Food Editor: Rachel Blackmore
Assistant Food Editor: Anneka Mitchell
Home Economist: Donna Hay
Editorial Coordinator: Margaret Kelly
Subeditor: Ella Martin

PHOTOGRAPHY
Ashley Mackevicius

STYLING
Carolyn Fienberg
Wendy Berecry (cover)

DESIGN AND PRODUCTION
Manager: Sheridan Carter
Layout: Tara Barrett
Finished Art: Stephen Joseph
Cover Design: Frank Pithers

PUBLISHER
Philippa Sandall

Includes Index
ISBN 1 85391 248 4
ISBN 1 86343 079 2 (pbk)

Published by J.B. Fairfax Press Pty Ltd
80-82 McLachlan Avenue
Rushcutters Bay 2011

Formatted by J.B. Fairfax Press Pty Ltd
Output by Adtype, Sydney
Printed by Toppan Printing Co.
Hong Kong

Distributed by J.B. Fairfax Press Pty Ltd
9 Trinity Centre, Park Farm Estate
Wellingborough, Northants
Ph: (0933) 402330 Fax: (0933) 402234

Barbecuing is one of the simplest and friendliest ways to entertain. No longer do you need to leave barbecuing to chance. This book, filled with wonderful ideas, recipes and menus, will ensure that every barbecue is a raging success.

This book has been divided into two sections: Barbecue Occasions, in which the recipes have been grouped together around a theme, and Barbecue Basics, filled with easy ideas and recipes to make that piece of steak or those lamb chops something special.

So turn the pages, choose your menu, light the barbecue and enjoy the wonderful flavour of food cooked in the outdoors.

CONTENTS

THE PANTRY SHELF

Unless otherwise stated the following ingredients used in this book are:

Cream	Double, suitable for whipping
Flour	White flour, plain or standard
Sugar	White sugar

WHAT'S IN A TABLESPOON?

AUSTRALIA
1 tablespoon   20 mL   4 teaspoons

NEW ZEALAND
1 tablespoon   15 mL   3 teaspoons

UNITED KINGDOM
1 tablespoon   15 mL   3 teaspoons

The recipes in this book were tested in Australia where a 20 mL tablespoon is standard. All measures are level.

The tablespoon in the New Zealand and United Kingdom set of measuring spoons is 15 mL. In many recipes this difference will not matter. For recipes using baking powder, gelatine, bicarbonate of soda, or small quantities of flour and cornflour, simply add another teaspoon for each tablespoon specified.

CANNED FOODS

Can sizes vary between countries and manufacturers. You may find the quantities in this book are slightly different from what is available. Purchase and use the can size nearest to the suggested size in the recipe.

BARBECUE OCCASIONS

The easy informality of a barbecue is one of the simplest and friendliest ways to entertain. In this section you will find a host of ideas for your next barbecue party. The dishes in the menus have been designed to go together, but do not feel that you have to cook everything. Adjust the quantities and number of dishes according to the size of your party.

So often a barbecue is left to chance and at the last minute it is realised that the steaks are not marinated, the fire is not hot enough and the beer not chilled. The secret to success is organisation. Be-

cause of its casual nature a barbecue party is the ideal time to involve family and friends, but you will probably need to check that each person has done their job. It is useful to draw up a work plan, so that the barbecue is lit in plenty of time and the food and drink is ready when it should be.

Also, check the area where you plan to hold the party. Is there plenty of room for the cooking to take place? Are there enough places for people to sit or do you need to get chairs from friends or elsewhere? Is there somewhere to serve the drinks and where are the salads and accompaniments going to go?

The smell of food being cooked on a barbecue always seems to whet appetites, so remember to supply snacks that can be eaten while the steaks and chops are cooking. In the first part of this book you will find Pitta Crisps, Crudités with Herb Mayonnaise and many more ideas to stave off the hunger pangs before the *real* food is ready.

With the large range of barbecue cookers now available it is possible for just about anyone to own one and so be able to entertain in this easy, fun way.

Fast Food

Hamburgers, ham and cheese skewers, and a salad bar make this the perfect barbecue for a mixed-age group. Bake potatoes on the barbecue for an hour to complete the meal.

Best Ever Hamburgers
(recipe page 8)

White china The Bay Tree Table Modern Living

PITTA CRISPS

These easy-to-make snacks are great to nibble on while waiting for the barbecue food to cook.

Serves 10
Oven temperature 200°C, 400°F, Gas 6

- [ ] **6 pitta bread**
- [ ] **4 tablespoons vegetable oil**
- [ ] **60 g/2 oz grated Parmesan cheese**
- [ ] **2 teaspoons paprika**
- [ ] **1/2 teaspoon chilli powder**

1 Split each pitta bread in half, horizontally, brush with oil and place on baking trays.

2 Place Parmesan cheese, paprika and chilli in a small bowl and mix to combine. Sprinkle bread with cheese mixture and bake for 15 minutes or until bread is crisp. Allow bread to cool, then break into pieces.

HAM AND CHEESE SKEWERS

Grilled ham and cheese sandwiches on a skewer!

Makes 10 skewers

- [ ] **250 g/8 oz sliced ham, cut into strips 3 cm/1 1/4 in wide**
- [ ] **375 g/12 oz tasty cheese (mature Cheddar) cut into 1 cm/1/2 in cubes**
- [ ] **1 loaf wholegrain bread, cut into 1 cm/1/2 in cubes**
- [ ] **10 skewers, lightly oiled**

1 Preheat barbecue to a medium heat.

2 Wrap ham strips around cheese cubes. Thread ham-wrapped cheese cubes and bread cubes, alternately, on to skewers.

3 Cook on lightly oiled barbecue grill, turning frequently, for 4-5 minutes or until bread is toasted and cheese just starts to melt.

Chilli Honey Drumsticks, Ham and Cheese Skewers, Pitta Crisps

BEST EVER HAMBURGERS

Serve the patties and rolls separately and allow people to make their own hamburger using the salad bar ingredients.

Makes 10 burgers

- [ ] **10 wholemeal rolls, split in half**

MEAT PATTIES
- [ ] **1 kg/2 lb lean minced beef**
- [ ] **1 onion, finely chopped**
- [ ] **1 carrot, grated**
- [ ] **2 cups/60 g/2 oz bread crumbs, made from stale bread**
- [ ] **1 tablespoon Worcestershire sauce**
- [ ] **1 tablespoon tomato sauce**
- [ ] **dash chilli sauce, according to taste**
- [ ] **2 tablespoons finely chopped fresh parsley**
- [ ] **freshly ground black pepper**

1 Preheat barbecue to a medium heat. To make patties, place beef, onion, carrot, bread crumbs, Worcestershire sauce, tomato sauce, chilli sauce, parsley and black pepper to taste in a bowl, and mix to combine.

2 Wet hands and shape meat mixture into ten patties. Place patties on a tray, cover and refrigerate until ready to cook.

3 Cook patties on lightly oiled barbecue plate (griddle), or in a lightly oiled frying pan on the barbecue, for 4-5 minutes each side or until cooked to your liking, pressing down with a spatula during cooking. Toast rolls on barbecue.

Burgers with onions: Onions can be cooked at the same time as the burgers. Allowing 1 onion for every 2 people, slice onions and cook with a little oil on barbecue plate (griddle) or in a frying pan.

Hamburgers with hidden fillings: It is fun and easy to make hamburgers that hold a surprise. Cheese is always a popular hidden ingredient – you might like to try tasty cheese (mature Cheddar), mozzarella or blue cheese. Simply cut cheese into 2.5 cm/1 in cubes and, when shaping your pattie, place cheese in centre of pattie and shape meat around it.

CHILLI HONEY DRUMSTICKS

Serves 10

- [ ] **10 chicken drumsticks**

CHILLI HONEY MARINADE
- [ ] **1/2 cup/125 mL/4 fl oz lemon juice**
- [ ] **1/2 cup/170 g/5 1/2 oz honey**

Plates Modern Living *Plants* Balmain Garden Centre *Basket* Parterre Garden

- □ **1 clove garlic, crushed**
- □ **pinch chilli powder**

1   To make marinade, place lemon juice, honey, garlic and chilli powder in a bowl and mix to combine.

2   Place drumsticks in a shallow glass or ceramic dish, pour marinade over and toss to coat. Cover and marinate in the refrigerator for at least 2 hours, or overnight, turning several times during marinating.

3   Preheat barbecue to a medium heat. Drain drumsticks and reserve marinade. Cook drumsticks on lightly oiled barbecue, brushing frequently with marinade for 10-15 minutes, or until chicken is tender.

Salad Bar

Arranging a salad bar that includes bowls of salad ingredients and toppings for potatoes is a great way of allowing people to assemble their own hamburgers, make their own salads and choose their favourite toppings for baked potatoes.

Quantities will vary depending on who you are feeding, but remember that appetites seem to increase outdoors.

SALAD BOWLS

- □ **mixed lettuce leaves**
- □ **tomato slices or halved cherry tomatoes**
- □ **beetroot slices**
- □ **sliced cucumbers**
- □ **tasty cheese (mature Cheddar) slices**
- □ **sliced red and green peppers**
- □ **hard-boiled eggs, sliced**
- □ **chopped spring onions**
- □ **sliced raw mushrooms**
- □ **grated raw carrot**

POTATO TOPPERS

- □ **snipped chives**
- □ **sour cream**
- □ **bacon pieces**
- □ **grated tasty cheese (mature Cheddar)**

PICKLES AND SAUCES

- □ **tomato sauce**
- □ **mustard pickle**
- □ **barbecue sauce**
- □ **Worcestershire sauce**
- □ **selection of mustards**

FRUIT AND NUTS

Fruit and nuts provide a healthy and delicious snack to eat while waiting for the barbecued food and make a good alternative for dessert.

- □ **melon slices**
- □ **orange segments**
- □ **kiwifruit slices**
- □ **fresh pineapple wedges or slices**
- □ **bananas, whole or sliced and tossed in lemon juice**
- □ **apples, whole or cubed and tossed in lemon juice**
- □ **selection dried fruit and nuts**

MARSHMALLOW SURPRISES

Eat with care – these delicious morsels are very hot when first assembled.

Serves 10

- [ ] **20 plain biscuits**
- [ ] **20 white marshmallows**
- [ ] **20 pink marshmallows**
- [ ] **20 squares chocolate, broken into 10 pieces**

1   Preheat barbecue to a low heat. Top 10 biscuits with a chocolate piece.

2   Thread 1 white and 1 pink marshmallow onto a long-handled fork or skewer and toast slowly over barbecue so that the marshmallow is hot and gooey in the centre. Using a spoon, push marshmallows onto chocolate-topped biscuits and top with remaining biscuits. Press biscuits together and eat!

PUFF TOMATO AND MUSHROOM PIZZA

This easy pizza will keep hunger pangs at bay while your food is cooking on the barbecue.

Serves 8
Oven temperature 200°C, 400°F, Gas 6

- [ ] **375 g/12 oz prepared puff pastry**
- [ ] **60 g/2 oz fresh Parmesan cheese, grated**
- [ ] **125 g/4 oz mozzarella cheese, grated**
- [ ] **1 onion, finely sliced**
- [ ] **200 g/6¹/₂ oz mushrooms, sliced**
- [ ] **3 tomatoes, cut into 1 cm/¹/₂ in slices**
- [ ] **10 pitted black olives**
- [ ] **2 teaspoons chopped fresh oregano or ¹/₂ teaspoon dried oregano**
- [ ] **2 teaspoons chopped fresh thyme, or ¹/₂ teaspoon dried thyme**

1   Roll out pastry to fit a greased 26 x 32 cm/10¹/₂ x 12³/₄ in Swiss roll tin. Sprinkle pastry with Parmesan and mozzarella cheeses, then top with onion, mushrooms, tomatoes and olives. Sprinkle with oregano and thyme.

2   Bake for 30 minutes or until pastry is puffed and golden. Serve hot, warm or cold.

Above: Puff Tomato and Mushroom Pizza
Right: Marshmallow Surprises

Patio
Party

The barbecue takes the hard
work out of this party. Food is prepared
in advance so only the barbecue cooking
is done at the party. You spend less
time in the kitchen and more time
with your guests.

*Barbecued Beef
on Béarnaise Bread
(recipe page 14)*

BARBECUED BEEF ON BEARNAISE BREAD

Slices of freshly barbecued beef combine with warm bread to make this tasty, hot, open sandwich.

Serves 10

- [ ] **750 g/1 1/2 lb beef fillet**
- [ ] **1 tablespoon fresh tarragon or 1 teaspoon dried tarragon**
- [ ] **2 tablespoons vegetable oil**
- [ ] **3 tablespoons white wine**
- [ ] **1 bread stick, cut into slices**
- [ ] **6 tablespoons finely chopped fresh parsley**

BEARNAISE BUTTER

- [ ] **3 tablespoons white wine vinegar**
- [ ] **3 tablespoons white wine**
- [ ] **3 spring onions, finely chopped**
- [ ] **1 tablespoon fresh tarragon or 1 teaspoon dried tarragon**
- [ ] **125 g/4 oz butter, at room temperature, cut into pieces**
- [ ] **freshly ground black pepper**

1   Trim meat of all visible fat. Tie with string at even intervals so that meat retains its shape during cooking, then place in a shallow glass or ceramic dish. Place tarragon, oil and wine in a small bowl and mix to combine. Pour over meat in dish, cover and marinate in refrigerator overnight. Turn occasionally during marinating.

2   To make Béarnaise Butter, place vinegar, wine, spring onions and tarragon in a small saucepan and bring to the boil, then reduce heat and simmer until liquid is reduced to 2 tablespoons. Remove from heat and set aside to cool completely. Place butter, cold vinegar mixture and black pepper to taste in a food processor and process until butter is combined and smooth. Spread one side of each bread slice with Béarnaise Butter, then reassemble loaf and wrap in a double thickness of aluminium foil. Refrigerate until required.

3   Preheat barbecue to a high heat. Drain beef and sear on all sides, on lightly oiled barbecue. Move fillet to a cooler section of the barbecue and cook, turning frequently,

for 15-20 minutes or until cooked to your liking. Place beef on side of barbecue to keep warm. Place foil-wrapped bread on barbecue and heat for 10 minutes or until bread is warmed through.

To serve: Thinly slice beef and place on slices of warm bread. Arrange on a large platter with a bowl of finely chopped parsley and a pepper grinder. Serve immediately. Each person helps themselves to an open sandwich and adds parsley and black pepper to taste.

Do ahead: Much of this dish can be prepared ahead of time leaving only the cooking of the beef and the warming of the bread to be done at the time of the barbecue. Place the beef into the marinade the night before you are going to cook it. The bread can be made up and refrigerated or frozen until required. Allow the frozen loaf to defrost at room temperature for 1-2 hours before heating through.

CRUDITES WITH HERB MAYONNAISE

Serves 10

- [ ] **a selection of vegetables such as broccoli and cauliflower florets, carrot sticks and baby new potatoes**

HERB MAYONNAISE
- [ ] **30 g/1 oz fresh parsley sprigs**
- [ ] **30 g/1 oz fresh basil leaves**
- [ ] **1/2 cup/125 g/4 oz mayonnaise**
- [ ] **1/3 cup/90 g/ 3 oz sour cream**
- [ ] **2 teaspoons French mustard**
- [ ] **freshly ground black pepper**

1 Steam or microwave vegetables separately until just tender. Drain, refresh under cold running water, drain and set aside.

2 To make mayonnaise, place parsley and basil in a food processor or blender and process to finely chop. Add mayonnaise, sour cream, mustard and black pepper to taste and process to combine.

To serve: Arrange vegetables on a large platter and accompany with Herb Mayonnaise.

Cook's tip: This mayonnaise is delicious served with any lightly cooked or steamed vegetables. You might like to try serving snow peas (mangetout), zucchini (courgettes), asparagus or cucumber on this platter instead of, or as well as, the vegetables that are suggested in the recipe.

SMOKED SALMON AND WATERCRESS ROULADE

Serves 10
Oven temperature 180°C, 350°F, Gas 4

- [ ] **1 bunch/90 g/3 oz watercress**
- [ ] **1 teaspoon finely chopped fresh parsley**
- [ ] **2 eggs, separated**
- [ ] **2 tablespoons flour**
- [ ] **freshly ground black pepper**

SMOKED SALMON FILLING
- [ ] **60 g/2 oz cream cheese**
- [ ] **2 tablespoons sour cream**
- [ ] **90 g/3 oz smoked salmon**
- [ ] **1 teaspoon lemon juice**

- [ ] **1 1/2 teaspoons gelatine dissolved in 1 1/2 tablespoons hot water, cooled**

1 Place watercress leaves, parsley, egg yolks, flour and pepper to taste in a food processor and process until mixture is smooth. Transfer watercress mixture to a bowl. Place egg whites in a bowl and beat until stiff peaks form. Fold egg white mixture into watercress mixture.

2 Spoon roulade mixture into a greased and lined 26 x 32 cm/10 1/2 x 12 3/4 in Swiss roll tin and bake for 5 minutes or until just cooked. Turn roulade onto a damp teatowel and roll up from short side. Set aside to cool.

3 To make filling, place cream cheese, sour cream, smoked salmon and lemon juice in a food processor and process until mixture is smooth. Stir gelatine mixture into smoked salmon mixture.

4 Unroll cold roulade, spread with filling and reroll. Cover and chill. Cut into slices to serve.

Left: Smoked Salmon and Watercress Roulade
Above: Crudités with Herb Mayonnaise

FRUIT AND CHEESE PLATTER

Choose fruit in season and arrange with your favourite cheeses on a large platter.

Serves 10

- [ ] **3 tablespoons fresh lemon juice**
- [ ] **2 red-skinned apples, cored and cut into wedges**
- [ ] **2 green-skinned apples, cored and cut into wedges**
- [ ] **4 kiwifruit, peeled and cut into slices**
- [ ] **2 oranges, peeled, segmented and white pith removed**
- [ ] **100 g/4 oz Camembert cheese**
- [ ] **100 g/4 oz Stilton cheese**
- [ ] **100 g/4 oz tasty cheese (mature Cheddar), choose your favourite brand**
- [ ] **cheese biscuits, purchased or homemade (see recipe)**
- [ ] **Passion Fruit Yogurt Dip (see recipe)**

1 Place lemon juice in a small bowl, add red and green apple wedges and toss to coat. This will help prevent the apple wedges from going brown.

2 Arrange red and green apple wedges, kiwifruit slices, orange segments, Camembert, Stilton and tasty (mature Cheddar) cheeses attractively with biscuits and dip on a large platter.

HERB AND CHEESE BISCUITS

Makes 30
Oven temperature 200°C, 400°F, Gas 6

- [ ] **125 g/4 oz butter**
- [ ] **1¹/₂ cups/185 g/6 oz flour, sifted**
- [ ] **freshly ground black pepper**
- [ ] **45 g/1¹/₂ oz grated tasty cheese (mature Cheddar)**
- [ ] **1 tablespoon snipped fresh chives**
- [ ] **1 tablespoon finely chopped fresh parsley**
- [ ] **pinch chilli powder**
- [ ] **pinch mustard powder**
- [ ] **2 eggs, lightly beaten**

1 Place butter, flour and black pepper to taste in a food processor and process until mixture resembles fine bread crumbs. Add cheese, chives, parsley, chilli and mustard powders, and process to combine. With machine running, slowly add egg until dough binds.

2 Turn dough onto a floured surface and knead lightly until smooth. Wrap in plastic food wrap and refrigerate for 20 minutes.

3 Roll dough out on a lightly floured surface to 3 mm/¹/₈ in in thickness and, using a fluted 5 cm/2 in biscuit cutter, cut out rounds of dough. Place on a lightly greased baking tray and bake for 8-10 minutes or until golden. Stand on trays for 5 minutes before removing to wire racks to cool completely.

PASSION FRUIT YOGURT DIP

The perfect accompaniment to any fresh fruit.

Makes 2 cups/400 g/12¹/₂ oz

- [ ] **2 cups/400 g/12¹/₂ oz unsweetened natural yogurt**
- [ ] **2 tablespoons honey**
- [ ] **3 tablespoons passion fruit pulp or pulp 4-5 passion fruit**

Place yogurt, honey and passion fruit pulp in a bowl and mix to combine.

Plates Villa Italiana *Fabric* Les Olivades *Table* Mondo Cane

BARBECUED MUSHROOMS WITH CHILLI BUTTER

These delicious bite-sized morsels will disappear as fast as you can cook them.

Makes 20

☐ **20 button mushrooms, stalks removed**

CHILLI BUTTER
☐ **60 g/2 oz butter, at room temperature**

☐ **$^1/_2$ fresh red chilli, finely chopped**
☐ **$^1/_2$ teaspoon ground cumin**
☐ **1 tablespoon finely chopped fresh parsley**

1 To make Chilli Butter, place butter, chilli, cumin and parsley in a food processor or blender and process until combined and smooth. Chill until required.

2 Preheat barbecue to a high heat. Cut butter log into 20 pieces. Place a piece of butter on each mushroom and cook on lightly oiled barbecue for 4-5 minutes, or until butter melts and mushrooms are cooked. Serve immediately with toothpicks so that your guests can spear a mushroom then eat it.

Left: Fruit and Cheese Platter with Herb and Cheese Biscuits and Passion Fruit Yogurt Dip Above: Bite-sized Kebabs (recipes page 18), Barbecued Mushrooms with Chilli Butter

17

BITE-SIZED KEBABS

Skewers should be long enough so you do not burn your fingers during the cooking.

Each recipe is enough for 10 skewers

- [ ] **10 lightly oiled bamboo skewers**

CUCUMBER AND SCALLOPS
- [ ] **1 clove garlic, crushed**
- [ ] **1 spring onion, finely chopped**
- [ ] **1 tablespoon finely chopped fresh basil**
- [ ] **1 tablespoon olive oil**
- [ ] **2 tablespoons white wine vinegar**
- [ ] **freshly ground black pepper**
- [ ] **10 scallops, cleaned, or 1 firm white fish fillet cut into 2.5 cm/1 in cubes**
- [ ] **10 thin slices cucumber, skin left on**

1 Place garlic, spring onion, basil, oil, vinegar and black pepper to taste in a bowl and whisk to combine. Add scallops or fish pieces and cucumber slices and toss to coat then set aside to marinate for 30 minutes.

2 Preheat barbecue to a high heat. Drain scallops, or fish pieces, and cucumber, reserving marinade. Top each cucumber slice with a scallop or fish piece and thread a bamboo skewer through the cucumber and scallop or fish piece so that the cucumber folds halfway around the scallop or fish. Brush with reserved marinade and cook on lightly oiled barbecue, turning several times, for 2-3 minutes or until scallops or fish pieces are cooked.

CHICKEN AND MUSHROOMS
- [ ] **1 tablespoon lime or lemon juice**
- [ ] **1 tablespoon vegetable oil**
- [ ] **pinch chilli powder**
- [ ] **1 chicken breast fillet, skin removed, cut into 10 cubes**
- [ ] **5 button mushrooms, halved**

1 Place lime or lemon juice, oil and chilli powder in a bowl and mix to combine. Add chicken and mushroom halves and toss to combine. Set aside to marinate for 30 minutes.

2 Preheat barbecue to a high heat. Drain chicken and mushrooms, reserving marinade. Thread a chicken cube and a mushroom half onto each bamboo skewer. Brush with reserved marinade and cook on lightly oiled barbecue, turning several times, for 4-5 minutes or until chicken is cooked.

BACON AND PRAWNS
- [ ] **1 tablespoon Dijon mustard**
- [ ] **1 clove garlic, crushed**
- [ ] **1/4 red pepper, finely chopped**
- [ ] **1 tablespoon finely chopped fresh dill**
- [ ] **2 tablespoons olive oil**
- [ ] **2 tablespoons lemon juice**
- [ ] **freshly ground black pepper**
- [ ] **10 large cooked prawns, shelled with tails left intact**
- [ ] **4 rashers lean bacon, cut into ten 7.5 cm/3 in strips**

1 Place mustard, garlic, red pepper, dill, oil, lemon juice and black pepper to taste in a bowl and mix to combine. Add prawns and toss to coat. Set aside to marinate for 30 minutes.

2 Preheat barbecue to a high heat. Drain prawns and reserve marinade. Wrap a strip of bacon around each prawn and thread onto bamboo skewers. Brush with reserved marinade and cook on lightly oiled barbecue, turning several times, for 2-3 minutes or until bacon is cooked and crisp.

White Strawberry Sangria, Champagne Cocktail

THE COCKTAIL BAR

A cocktail party is an opportunity to offer some exciting and interesting drinks. If you are offering a large variety of drinks it is often easier to make only one or two drinks at a time. However, if you intend to offer only one or two different cocktails, the base can be made up in quantity to make mixing quicker and easier.

Tropical Passion

*Raspberry Cooler,
Virgin Island*

VIRGIN ISLAND

Makes 1 drink

- ☐ **1 slice fresh or canned pineapple, chopped**
- ☐ **¹/₂ cup/125 mL/4 fl oz pineapple juice**
- ☐ **2 tablespoons coconut milk**
- ☐ **1 tablespoon lemon juice**

Place pineapple, pineapple juice, coconut milk and lemon juice in a blender and blend until smooth. Fill a goblet with ice and pour pineapple mixture over ice.

CHAMPAGNE COCKTAIL

Makes 1 drink

- ☐ **1 tablespoon orange liqueur**
- ☐ **¹/₂ cup/125 mL/4 fl oz champagne**

Pour liqueur into a champagne glass and top with champagne.

WHITE STRAWBERRY SANGRIA

Makes 1 drink

- ☐ **4 strawberries**
- ☐ **1 tablespoon orange juice**
- ☐ **1 tablespoon orange liqueur**
- ☐ **¹/₂ cup/125 mL/4 fl oz white wine**
- ☐ **1 teaspoon sugar**

Place strawberries, orange juice, liqueur, wine and sugar in a blender and blend until smooth. Chill and pour into a chilled, large wine glass. Serve immediately.

TROPICAL PASSION

Makes 1 drink

- ☐ **¹/₄ cup/45 g/1¹/₂ oz chopped fresh or canned mango flesh**
- ☐ **2 tablespoons peach liqueur**
- ☐ **1 tablespoon cream (single)**
- ☐ **2-3 ice cubes**
- ☐ **¹/₂ cup/125 mL/4 fl oz lemonade**

Place mango, liqueur and cream in a blender and blend until smooth. Place ice in a large wine glass, pour mango mixture over, top with lemonade, stir and serve.

RASPBERRY COOLER

Makes 1 drink

- ☐ **125 g/4 oz fresh or frozen raspberries**
- ☐ **¹/₄ cup/60 mL/2 fl oz orange juice**
- ☐ **1 tablespoon lime juice**
- ☐ **1 tablespoon sugar**

Place raspberries, orange juice, lime juice and sugar in a blender and blend until smooth. Strain through a fine sieve and discard seeds. Fill a cocktail glass with ice and pour raspberry mixture over ice.

Thai Tastes

Chilli, coriander, ginger and garlic are the flavours of Thai cuisine. This Thai-flavoured menu cooked on the barbecue is sure to be a hit at your next party.

Oriental Rice Salad,
Mixed Satays,
Pickled Vegetables
(recipes pages 22 and 23)

Table Modern Living

WARM THAI BEEF SALAD

Traditionally the meat for this dish should be cooked rare.

Serves 8

- [ ] 1 kg/2 lb rump steak, cut into 2.5 cm/1 in thick steaks
- [ ] 1 cucumber, peeled and thinly sliced
- [ ] fresh coriander leaves, for garnishing
- [ ] 1 fresh red chilli, sliced

CORIANDER MARINADE
- [ ] 4 tablespoons soy sauce
- [ ] 2 tablespoons vegetable oil
- [ ] 1 teaspoon ground coriander
- [ ] 1 tablespoon finely chopped fresh coriander
- [ ] 1 tablespoon brown sugar
- [ ] freshly ground black pepper

1 Place steaks in a shallow glass or ceramic dish. To make marinade, place soy sauce, oil, ground and fresh coriander, sugar, and black pepper to taste in a small bowl and mix to combine. Pour marinade over meat in dish, cover and set aside to marinate for at least 1 hour. Arrange overlapping cucumber slices on a large platter, cover and refrigerate until required.

2 Preheat barbecue to a high heat. Drain steaks and reserve marinade. Sear steaks, on lightly oiled barbecue, for 1 minute each side. Move steaks to a cooler section of barbecue and cook for 3 minutes each side or until cooked to your liking. Place reserved marinade in a small saucepan, bring to the boil and cook for 3-4 minutes. Thinly slice steaks, arrange on top of cucumber, spoon over marinade and garnish with coriander leaves and sliced fresh chilli.

PICKLED VEGETABLES

Serve these vegetables hot, warm or cold. If making ahead of time, store in sterilised jars in the refrigerator for up to two weeks.

Serves 8

- [ ] 3 cups/750 mL/1¼ pt white vinegar
- [ ] 2 tablespoons sugar
- [ ] 2 teaspoons salt
- [ ] 1 large cucumber, peeled, seeds removed and cubed
- [ ] 1 small head cauliflower, cut into small florets
- [ ] 2 large carrots, sliced
- [ ] 1 head broccoli, cut into small florets
- [ ] 1 red pepper, cut into cubes
- [ ] 1 green pepper, cut into cubes
- [ ] 440 g/14 oz canned baby corn, drained
- [ ] 2 cloves garlic, chopped
- [ ] 1 large onion, chopped
- [ ] 3 dried red chillies, seeded and finely chopped
- [ ] 3 tablespoons vegetable oil
- [ ] 1 tablespoon sesame seeds, toasted

1 Place vinegar, sugar and salt in a large saucepan, bring to the boil and add cucumber, cauliflower, carrots, broccoli, red and green pepper and corn. Cook for 1 minute, then remove from heat and set aside to cool.

2 Place garlic, onion and chillies in a food processor or blender and process to make a paste. Heat oil in a large frying pan and cook garlic paste for 2-3 minutes, then add vegetables, vinegar mixture and sesame seeds. Cook for 1 minute longer and serve immediately, or spoon into sterilised jars and seal.

ORIENTAL RICE SALAD

Serves 8

- [ ] 125 g/4 oz long grain white rice
- [ ] 125 g/4 oz quick-cooking brown rice
- [ ] 125 g/4 oz wild rice
- [ ] 1 tablespoon vegetable oil
- [ ] 2 cloves garlic, crushed
- [ ] 4 spring onions, chopped
- [ ] 125 g/4 oz snow peas (mangetout)
- [ ] 90 g/3 oz unsalted cashews, toasted

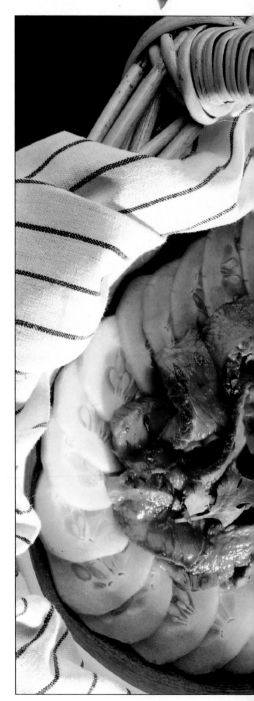

SESAME DRESSING

- ☐ **3 tablespoons brown vinegar**
- ☐ **2 teaspoons soy sauce**
- ☐ **1 teaspoon sesame oil**
- ☐ **¹/₂ teaspoon sugar**

1   Cook white, brown and wild rice, separately, in a large saucepan of boiling water following packet directions. Drain, and set aside to cool.

2   Heat oil in a frying pan and cook garlic and spring onions over a medium heat for 3-4 minutes or until onion softens. Add snow peas (mangetout) and cashews and cook for 3-4 minutes longer or until snow peas (mangetout) are just tender. Remove from heat and set aside to cool.

3   To make dressing, combine vinegar, soy sauce, oil and sugar in a screwtop jar and shake to combine.

4   Place white, brown and wild rice and snow pea (mangetout) mixture in a large salad bowl. Pour dressing over, toss to combine, cover and chill until required.

Warm Thai Beef Salad

MIXED SATAYS

Makes 12 skewers

- ☐ **250 g/8 oz chicken breast fillets, skin removed and sliced into thin strips, lengthwise**
- ☐ **250 g/8 oz beef fillet, sliced into thin strips, lengthwise**
- ☐ **250 g/8 oz pork fillet, sliced into thin strips, lengthwise**
- ☐ **12 skewers, lightly oiled**

CHILLI MARINADE
- ☐ **¹/₄ cup/60 mL/2 fl oz soy sauce**
- ☐ **2 tablespoons lime or lemon juice**
- ☐ **2 cloves garlic, crushed**
- ☐ **2 teaspoons finely grated fresh ginger**
- ☐ **1 fresh red chilli, finely chopped**
- ☐ **1 tablespoon finely chopped fresh coriander**

PEANUT SAUCE
- ☐ **¹/₂ cup/125 g/4 oz crunchy peanut butter**
- ☐ **1 onion, finely chopped**
- ☐ **2 tablespoons hoisin sauce**
- ☐ **2 cloves garlic, crushed**
- ☐ **¹/₂ cup/125 mL/4 fl oz coconut milk**
- ☐ **2 tablespoons finely chopped fresh coriander**

1   Weave chicken, beef and pork strips onto skewers and place in a shallow glass or ceramic dish.

2   To make marinade, place soy sauce, lime or lemon juice, garlic, ginger, chilli and coriander in a small bowl and mix to combine. Pour marinade over skewers in dish, cover and set aside to marinate for at least 1 hour.

3   Preheat barbecue to a medium heat. Cook kebabs on lightly oiled barbecue, turning frequently for 5-6 minutes, or until meats are cooked.

4   To make sauce, place peanut butter, onion, hoisin sauce, garlic and coconut milk in a food processor or blender and process until smooth. Stir in coriander. Serve with skewers for dipping.

HOT AND SOUR THAI STIR-FRY

Serves 8

- ☐ **2 tablespoons soy sauce**
- ☐ **1 tablespoon dry sherry**
- ☐ **1 fresh red chilli, seeded and finely chopped**
- ☐ **1 clove garlic, crushed**
- ☐ **500 g/1 lb tofu, cubed and drained**
- ☐ **1 tablespoon vegetable oil**
- ☐ **2 onions, sliced**
- ☐ **1 red pepper, cut into thin strips**
- ☐ **1 green pepper, cut into thin strips**
- ☐ **125 g/4 oz snow peas (mangetout), trimmed**
- ☐ **125 g/4 oz egg noodles, cooked and drained**
- ☐ **2 spring onions, finely chopped**
- ☐ **fresh coriander leaves, to garnish**

SPICY PEANUT SAUCE
- ☐ **2 cloves garlic, crushed**
- ☐ **¹/₂ cup/125 g/4 oz crunchy peanut butter**
- ☐ **3 tablespoons lime or lemon juice**
- ☐ **3 tablespoons soy sauce**
- ☐ **1 small fresh red chilli, finely chopped**
- ☐ **¹/₂ cup/125 mL/4 fl oz vegetable stock or water**

1   Preheat barbecue to a high heat. Place soy sauce, sherry, chilli and garlic in a bowl, and mix to combine. Add tofu, toss to coat and set aside to marinate for 30 minutes. Drain.

2   To make sauce, place garlic, peanut butter, lime or lemon juice, soy sauce and chilli in a food processor or blender and process to combine. With machine running, slowly add vegetable stock or water and process until combined.

3   Heat oil in a wok or frying pan on barbecue and stir-fry onions and red and green pepper for 4-5 minutes. Using a slotted spoon remove onions and peppers and set aside. Add tofu to wok and stir-fry for 1-2 minutes. Return onions and peppers to wok, add snow peas (mangetout) and noodles and stir-fry for 3-4 minutes longer. Add peanut sauce and toss to coat noodles and vegetables evenly with sauce. Transfer to a serving platter, garnish with spring onions and coriander leaves. Serve immediately.

MANGO ICE CREAM

Makes 1.5 litres/2½ pt

- [ ] **8 egg yolks**
- [ ] **1¼ cups/280 g/9 oz caster sugar**
- [ ] **4 cups/1 litre/1¾ pt milk**
- [ ] **2 cups/500 mL/16 fl oz cream (double)**
- [ ] **2 teaspoons vanilla essence**
- [ ] **250 g/8 oz mango, puréed**

1   Place egg yolks and sugar in a mixing bowl and beat until thick and creamy.

2   Place milk and cream in a large saucepan and bring just to the boil. Remove from heat and whisk gradually into egg yolk mixture. Return to pan and cook over a low heat, stirring constantly, until mixture coats the back of a wooden spoon.

3   Stir in vanilla essence and fold in mango purée. Transfer mixture to an ice cream maker and freeze according to the manufacturer's instructions.

Cook's tip: If you do not have an ice cream maker, place the custard mixture in a deep-sided metal container and freeze until the mixture begins to set around the edge. Then remove from freezer and beat with an electric mixer until smooth. To ensure a smooth texture, repeat this process 2-3 times more to prevent large ice crystals forming.

Left: Hot and Sour Thai Stir-Fry
Below: Mango Ice Cream

Plates The Bay Tree

Fresh Mangos

Cutting a mango is easy once you know how. The waste from around the stone can be used to make mango ice cream, or cut into cubes, tossed in lime or lemon juice and served as a side dish to the main meal. Allow half a mango per person for dessert.

1   Place the mango on a chopping board and, cutting as close as possible to the stone, cut a large slice from either side.

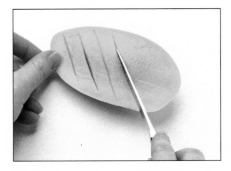

2   Taking one slice, cut the flesh into cubes, being careful not to cut the skin. Repeat with the other slice.

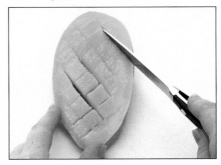

3   Turn the skin inside out. The flesh can now be easily removed from the skin and eaten.

Bow Tie Dinner

A special barbecue. Set a table on your patio or balcony, or in the garden, then cook and eat this barbecue together. Green beans tied in bundles and a crusty bread roll complete the meal.

*Bow Pasta Salad,
Char-grilled Mushrooms
and Toast, Beef with Bacon
Ties (recipes page 28)*

Plates and scarf Made Where Glasses Butler & Co

CHAR-GRILLED MUSHROOMS AND TOAST

This delicious first course takes only minutes to cook.

Serves 2

- ☐ 6 flat mushrooms
- ☐ 1/4 cup/60 mL/2 fl oz olive oil
- ☐ 2 thick slices of bread
- ☐ 1 clove garlic, cut in half
- ☐ 2 teaspoons finely chopped fresh parsley
- ☐ 2 teaspoons snipped fresh chives
- ☐ 1 teaspoon finely chopped fresh basil
- ☐ freshly ground black pepper

1   Preheat barbecue to a medium heat. Brush mushrooms with oil and cook on lightly oiled barbecue for 4-5 minutes or until cooked. Brush both sides of the bread with remaining oil and cook for 2-3 minutes each side or until golden.

2   Rub one side of each bread slice with cut side of garlic clove. Top each slice of bread with mushrooms, sprinkle with parsley, chives and basil. Season to taste with black pepper and serve immediately.

BEEF WITH BACON TIES

Serves 2

- ☐ 2 x 3 cm/1 1/4 in thick beef fillet steaks
- ☐ 2 rashers bacon, rind removed

CHILLI MARINADE
- ☐ 1 tablespoon vegetable oil
- ☐ 3 tablespoons sweet chilli sauce
- ☐ 1 tablespoon tomato paste (purée)
- ☐ 1 tablespoon teriyaki sauce
- ☐ freshly ground black pepper

1   To make marinade, place oil, chilli sauce, tomato paste (purée), teriyaki sauce and black pepper to taste in a bowl and mix to combine.

2   Place steaks in a shallow glass or ceramic dish. Pour marinade over and set aside to marinate for 2-3 hours, turning once.

3   Preheat barbecue to a high heat. Drain steaks and cook steak on lightly oiled barbecue plate (griddle) for 3-4 minutes each side or until cooked to your liking. Cook bacon rashers for 2-3 minutes, then wrap around each steak, bring ends together and tie a knot.

Serving suggestion: Green beans tied in bundles make an attractive accompaniment to this main course. To tie the beans use a long chive, or use a long thin strip of red pepper blanched in boiling water for 1 minute.

BOW PASTA SALAD

Serves 2

- ☐ 125 g/4 oz bow pasta
- ☐ 1/3 cup/90 mL/3 fl oz chicken stock
- ☐ 1 small leek, finely sliced
- ☐ 1 small zucchini (courgette), cut into thin strips
- ☐ 1 tablespoon pine nuts, toasted
- ☐ 1 tablespoon finely chopped fresh basil
- ☐ 1 tablespoon finely chopped fresh parsley

SUN-DRIED TOMATO SAUCE
- ☐ 3 sun-dried tomatoes, finely chopped
- ☐ 1 clove garlic, crushed
- ☐ 2 teaspoons pine nuts
- ☐ 1 tablespoon lemon juice
- ☐ 1/4 cup/60 mL/2 fl oz olive oil
- ☐ 1 tablespoon grated fresh Parmesan cheese
- ☐ freshly ground black pepper

1   To make sauce, place sun-dried tomatoes, garlic, pine nuts, lemon juice and 1 tablespoon oil in a food processor and process until smooth. With machine running, gradually add remaining oil. Mix in Parmesan cheese and season to taste with black pepper.

2   Cook pasta in boiling water in a saucepan following packet directions. Drain well and transfer to a bowl. Add sauce and toss to combine. Set aside to cool.

3   Place stock and leek in a nonstick frying pan and cook over a medium heat for 5 minutes or until leek softens. Add zucchini (courgette) and cook for 1 minute longer. Remove from heat, drain and set aside to cool. Add zucchini (courgette) mixture, pine nuts, basil and parsley to pasta and toss to combine. Cover and chill until required.

Glass bowl and table Modern Living

MINTED GREEN SALAD

Serves 2

- ☐ 1/4 honeydew melon
- ☐ 90 g/3 oz seedless green grapes
- ☐ 1 small Granny Smith apple, cored and sliced
- ☐ 1 kiwifruit, peeled and chopped

Salad Ideas

Many salads do not need a recipe if you have a few basic ingredients and an interesting dressing. Try some of the following ideas as accompaniments to your barbecued food.

Potato salad: Boil or microwave potatoes in their skins until tender. Drain, rinse under cold running water and set aside to cool. Cut potatoes in pieces – there is no need to peel. Place potatoes in a salad bowl with snipped chives, chopped parsley and chopped red or green pepper. Top with mayonnaise and toss to combine.

Quick lettuce salads are easy to make if you have 2 or 3 different types of lettuce and some fresh herbs. For the simplest salad of all, take a few leaves from each lettuce, wash and dry, tear into pieces and place in a salad bowl, add chopped fresh herbs and toss with a dressing. You might like to add chopped cucumber, chopped red or green pepper, chopped spring onions, diced celery or grated Parmesan cheese.

Coleslaw is easily made by shredding cabbage, combining it with grated carrot, diced red or green pepper, diced celery and chopped fresh herbs, then tossing through a dressing.

Tomato salad: There are a number of different tomato salads that you might like to make. Choose large ripe tomatoes, peel and cut into slices. Present these salads on a large platter with a raised edge. To make a tomato and basil salad, layer tomatoes on a serving platter, sprinkle with torn basil leaves and a vinaigrette dressing. Set aside to allow flavours to develop. To make a tomato and cucumber salad, layer sliced tomatoes and sliced cucumber on a platter, sprinkle with chopped fresh mint and vinaigrette dressing. A tomato and mozzarella salad is also a delicious barbecue salad. Layer slices of tomato and mozzarella cheese on a serving platter, sprinkle with snipped chives and a vinaigrette dressing.

MINT SYRUP
- ☐ **2 tablespoons sugar**
- ☐ **3 tablespoons water**
- ☐ **2 tablespoons mint liqueur**

1   To make syrup, place sugar, water and liqueur in a saucepan and cook, stirring over a medium heat until sugar dissolves. Bring to the boil, reduce heat and simmer for 2-3 minutes. Set aside to cool.

2   Remove seeds from melon and scoop out flesh using a melon baller. Place melon balls in a bowl. Separate grapes from stems and place in bowl. Add apple, kiwifruit and mint to bowl. Pour cooled syrup over fruit and toss to combine. Cover and chill until required.

Minted Green Salad

Hot & Spicy

Chillies, cilantro – or fresh coriander as we call it – avocado and limes are some of the ingredients that give Mexican food its wonderful flavours and distinctive taste.

Hot Chilli Pork Spareribs,
Margaritas
(recipes page 32)

Plates Villa Italiana Glasses The Bay Tree Napkin Modern Living Plants Balmain Garden Centre

HOT CHILLI PORK SPARERIBS

Apple, pork and chilli combine for the tastiest spareribs ever.

Serves 6

- ☐ **6 small pork back rib racks**
- ☐ **freshly ground black pepper**
- ☐ **¹/₂ cup/125 mL/4 fl oz apple juice**
- ☐ **¹/₄ cup/60 mL/2 fl oz lime juice**
- ☐ **dash Tabasco sauce**

APPLE CHILLI GLAZE
- ☐ **1 tablespoons vegetable oil**
- ☐ **2 onions, finely chopped**
- ☐ **2 cloves garlic, crushed**
- ☐ **1 fresh red chilli, seeded and finely chopped**
- ☐ **125 g/4 oz canned apple purée**
- ☐ **1 cup/315 g/10 oz apple jelly**
- ☐ **¹/₂ cup/125 mL/4 fl oz apple juice**
- ☐ **2 tablespoons lime juice**
- ☐ **freshly ground black pepper**

1 Season ribs with black pepper and place in a shallow glass or ceramic dish. Combine apple juice, lime juice and Tabasco sauce, pour over ribs and toss to coat. Cover and refrigerate for 1-2 hours.

2 To make glaze, heat oil in a saucepan and cook onions, garlic and chilli over a medium heat for 10 minutes or until onions are soft. Stir in apple purée, jelly and juice, bring to simmering and simmer, stirring frequently, for 15 minutes or until mixture thickens. Stir in lime juice and season to taste with black pepper and cook for 15 minutes longer or until mixture thickens.

3 Preheat barbecue to a medium heat. Drain ribs and sear on lightly oiled barbecue for 5 minutes each side, brushing with reserved apple juice mixture frequently. Brush ribs with warm glaze and cook, turning, for 5 minutes longer. Serve ribs with remaining glaze.

MARGARITAS

This cool Mexican drink is perfect to serve with Mexican food. Start preparing the drink earlier in the day as the limes for the Lime Cooler need to steep for at least an hour.

Makes 12 drinks

- ☐ **4 cups/1 litre/1³/₄ pt Lime Cooler (see recipe)**
- ☐ **¹/₂ cup/125 mL/4 fl oz fresh lime juice**
- ☐ **pinch salt**
- ☐ **1¹/₂ cups/375 mL/12 fl oz tequila**
- ☐ **¹/₂ cup/125 mL/4 fl oz orange liqueur**
- ☐ **ice cubes**

1 To make margarita mixture, place Lime Cooler, lime juice, salt, tequila and liqueur in a large jug and mix to combine. Cover and set aside for 30 minutes, to allow the flavours to blend.

2 Just prior to serving, place 2 cups/500 mL/8 fl oz margarita mixture in a blender with ice cubes and blend for 30 seconds to chop ice. Mix blended margarita with remaining margarita, then pour into glasses and serve immediately.

Serving suggestion: Traditionally margaritas are served in salt-rimmed glasses. To salt the rim of a glass, dip it in lime juice then in salt.

Cook's tip: If you do not have a blender, just pour the margarita mixture over cracked or crushed ice.

LIME COOLER

This Lime Cooler makes a refreshing drink served over ice for those who prefer a nonalcoholic drink. It is important to choose underripe limes with dark green skins, so that the liquid has a green colour.

- ☐ **10 dark green limes**
- ☐ **4 cups/1 litre/1³/₄ pt water**
- ☐ **1 cup/250 g/8 oz sugar**

1 Finely grate lime rind into a bowl. Add water, cover and set aside to stand for 1 hour.

2 Strain mixture through a fine sieve, pressing rind to extract as much liquid as possible. Place liquid in a saucepan, add sugar and stir over a low heat until sugar dissolves. Cover and refrigerate until required.

Lime Ices: You might like to freeze this cooler to make refreshing lime ice blocks for summer days.

GUACAMOLE WITH TORTILLAS

Serves 6
Oven temperature 180°C, 350°F, Gas 4

- ☐ **6 corn tortillas**

CHILLI BUTTER
- ☐ **90 g/3 oz butter**
- ☐ **2 teaspoons finely grated lemon rind**
- ☐ **2 teaspoons sweet chilli sauce**
- ☐ **1 teaspoon ground cumin**

GUACAMOLE
- ☐ **1 avocado, halved, stoned and peeled**
- ☐ **1 tomato, peeled and finely chopped**
- ☐ **2 tablespoons lemon juice**
- ☐ **1 tablespoon finely chopped fresh coriander or parsley**

1 To make Chilli Butter, place butter, lemon rind, chilli sauce and cumin in a bowl and mix to combine.

2 To make Guacamole, place avocado in a bowl and mash with a fork. Stir in tomato, lemon juice and coriander or parsley.

3 Place tortillas in a single layer on a baking tray and heat in oven for 3-5 minutes or until warm.

To serve: Place Chilli Butter, Guacamole and tortillas on a platter so that each person can spread a tortilla with Chilli Butter, top with Guacamole, then roll up and eat.

CHEESE AND BACON NACHOS

Serves 6
Oven temperature 180°C, 350°F, Gas 4

- ☐ **6 rashers bacon, finely chopped**
- ☐ **6 spring onions, finely chopped**
- ☐ **4 jalapeño chillies, finely chopped**
- ☐ **200 g/6¹/₂ oz packet corn chips**
- ☐ **125 g/4 oz grated tasty cheese (mature Cheddar)**
- ☐ **1 cup/250 g/8 oz sour cream**

1   Cook bacon, spring onions and chillies in a nonstick frying pan over a medium heat for 4-5 minutes or until crisp. Remove from pan and drain on absorbent kitchen paper.

2   Place corn chips in a shallow oven-proof dish and sprinkle with bacon mixture and cheese. Bake for 5-8 minutes or until heated through and cheese is melted. Serve immediately, accompanied with sour cream for dipping.

Jalapeño chillies: These are the medium-to-dark green chillies that taper to a blunt end and are 5-7.5 cm/2-3 in long and 2-2.5 cm/³/₄-1 in wide. They are medium-to-hot in taste and are also available canned or bottled.

Guacamole with Tortillas,
Cheese and Bacon Nachos

Basket, platter, plates and bowl/ Corso de Fiori

SPICY CORN COBS

Serves 6

- ☐ **125 g/4 oz butter, softened**
- ☐ **1 small fresh red chilli, finely chopped**
- ☐ **2 tablespoons grated Parmesan cheese**
- ☐ **1 tablespoon finely chopped fresh coriander**
- ☐ **6 corn cobs, husks removed**

1 Place butter, chilli, Parmesan cheese and coriander in a food processor or blender and process until combined and smooth.

2 Preheat barbecue to a medium heat. Wrap corn cobs in a double thickness of aluminium foil and cook on barbecue for 30-35 minutes or until corn is tender. To serve, spread corn cobs with chilli butter.

BARBECUED BANANAS WITH CREAM

Serves 6

- ☐ **90 g/3 oz butter**
- ☐ **5 bananas, diagonally sliced**
- ☐ **$^1/_2$ cup/125 mL/4 fl oz dark rum**
- ☐ **$^1/_2$ teaspoon nutmeg**
- ☐ **$^1/_4$ cup/45 g/1$^1/_2$ oz brown sugar**
- ☐ **30 g/1 oz slivered almonds, toasted**

THICK CREAM
- ☐ **$^1/_2$ cup/125 g/4 oz sour cream**
- ☐ **2 tablespoons cream (double)**

1 To make Thick Cream, place sour cream and cream in a small bowl and mix to combine. Cover and refrigerate until required.

2 Preheat barbecue to a medium heat. Melt butter in a large frying pan on barbecue and cook bananas for 3-4 minutes or until golden brown. Remove bananas from pan and place on a warm serving dish.

3 Add rum, nutmeg and sugar to frying pan and cook, stirring, for 3-4 minutes or until a glaze forms. Pour over bananas and sprinkle with nuts. Serve immediately with Thick Cream.

SPICY CHICKEN FAJITAS

Serves 6

- ☐ **750 g/1¹/₂ lb chicken breast fillets, skin removed**
- ☐ **2 onions, finely sliced**
- ☐ **1 tablespoon vegetable oil**
- ☐ **1 avocado, stoned, peeled and diced**
- ☐ **3 tomatoes, peeled and diced**
- ☐ **6 spring onions, finely chopped**
- ☐ **1 cup/200 g/6¹/₂ oz natural yogurt**
- ☐ **60 g/2 oz grated tasty cheese (mature Cheddar)**
- ☐ **3 tablespoons chopped fresh coriander**
- ☐ **6 flour tortillas or tacos, warmed**

LIME MARINADE
- ☐ **¹/₂ cup/125 mL/4 fl oz lime juice**
- ☐ **¹/₂ cup/125 mL/4 fl oz vegetable oil**
- ☐ **1 fresh red chilli, seeded and finely chopped**

1   To make marinade, combine lime juice, oil and chilli. Place chicken breast fillets and onions in a shallow glass or ceramic dish and pour marinade over. Toss to coat, cover and set aside to marinate, turning occasionally, for 2-3 hours.

2   Preheat barbecue to a medium heat. Drain chicken and onions. Heat oil in a frying pan on barbecue and cook onions for 10-15 minutes or until golden. Cook chicken on lightly oiled barbecue, turning frequently, for 5-7 minutes or until cooked. Cut cooked chicken into strips.

3   To serve, place avocado, tomatoes, spring onions, cheese, yogurt and coriander in separate bowls. Arrange chicken strips, onions and tortillas or tacos on a large serving platter and allow each person to fill their own tortilla or taco to taste.

WARM BEAN AND VEGETABLE SALAD

Serves 6

- ☐ **1 red pepper**
- ☐ **1 green pepper**
- ☐ **1 red onion, finely chopped**
- ☐ **2 spring onions, finely chopped**
- ☐ **3 tomatoes, peeled and finely diced**
- ☐ **1 clove garlic, crushed**
- ☐ **1 dried red chilli, crushed**
- ☐ **750 g/1¹/₂ lb canned mixed beans, drained**
- ☐ **1 fresh red chilli, finely chopped**
- ☐ **2 tablespoons red wine vinegar**
- ☐ **1 tablespoon vegetable oil**
- ☐ **3 tablespoons finely chopped fresh coriander**
- ☐ **freshly ground black pepper**

1   Place red and green peppers under a hot grill or on a medium heat on lightly oiled barbecue and cook until skin blisters and chars. Remove from heat and place in a paper or plastic food bag and leave for 10 minutes or until cool enough to handle. Remove skins and cut peppers into strips.

2   Place red and green pepper strips, red onion, spring onions, tomatoes, garlic, beans, chilli and vinegar in a large bowl and toss to combine.

3   Preheat barbecue to a medium heat. Heat oil in a large frying pan on barbecue, add vegetable mixture and cook, stirring, for 4-5 minutes or until just warmed. Stir in coriander and season to taste with black pepper. Serve immediately.

Left: Warm Bean and Vegetable Salad, Spicy Chicken Fajitas, Spicy Corn Cobs
Right: Barbecued Bananas with Cream

Buffet Lunch

Ask your friends for Sunday lunch, set a table in the garden, light the barbecue and enjoy this delicious meal. The menu provides a variety of dishes that will cater to most tastes and can be easily adapted to suit vegetarians.

Brown Ale Damper, Chicken with Creamy Pesto Stuffing, Blue Cheese Caesar Salad (recipes page 38)

Table and basket Mondo Cane Glasses and jug Butler & Co Fabric Les Olivades Plants Balmain Garden Centre

BLUE CHEESE CAESAR SALAD

If cos lettuce is unavailable iceberg lettuce can be used instead.

Serves 10

- ☐ ¹/₃ cup/90 mL/3 fl oz olive oil
- ☐ 2 slices bread, crusts removed and cut into 1 cm/¹/₂ in cubes
- ☐ 2 rashers bacon, chopped
- ☐ 1 cos lettuce, washed, leaves separated, torn into large pieces
- ☐ 60 g/2 oz pine nuts, toasted
- ☐ 125 g/4 oz fresh Parmesan cheese, grated

BLUE CHEESE DRESSING
- ☐ 90 g/3 oz Stilton or blue cheese
- ☐ 2 tablespoons natural yogurt
- ☐ 2 tablespoons sour cream
- ☐ ¹/₃ cup/90 mL/3 fl oz cream (double)
- ☐ 2 tablespoons lemon juice
- ☐ freshly ground black pepper

1   To make croutons, heat oil in a frying pan and cook bread, tossing frequently, over a medium-high heat for 1-2 minutes or until golden on all sides. Remove from pan and drain on absorbent kitchen paper.

2   Place bacon in a nonstick frying pan and cook over a medium heat for 3-4 minutes or until crisp. Remove from pan and drain on absorbent kitchen paper.

3   To make dressing, place Stilton or blue cheese, yogurt, sour cream, cream, lemon juice and black pepper to taste in a food processor or blender and process until combined and mixture is smooth.

4   Place lettuce, bacon, croutons and pine nuts in a serving bowl, pour dressing over and toss. Sprinkle with Parmesan cheese and serve immediately.

CHICKEN WITH CREAMY PESTO STUFFING

Serves 10

- ☐ 3 x 1.5 kg/3 lb chickens

CREAMY PESTO STUFFING
- ☐ 90 g/3 oz basil leaves
- ☐ 60 g/2 oz pine nuts
- ☐ ¹/₂ cup/60 g/2 oz finely grated Parmesan cheese
- ☐ 250 g/8 oz cream cheese, softened

1   To make stuffing, place basil leaves, pine nuts and Parmesan cheese in a food processor and process to finely chopped. Stir basil mixture into cream cheese.

2   Cut through backbone of each chicken. Remove both halves of backbone, then turn chicken over and press to flatten.

3   Using your fingers or the handle of a wooden spoon, loosen skin over breasts, thighs and legs of chicken. Push stuffing under loosened skin, then thread skewers through wings and legs of chickens.

4   Preheat barbecue to a medium heat. Cook chicken on lightly oiled barbecue for 15-20 minutes each side or until chicken is cooked through.

When is the chicken cooked? To test your chicken for doneness pierce the thickest part of the chicken at the thigh joint and when the juices run clear the bird is cooked.

BROWN ALE DAMPER

Makes a 20 cm/8 in damper

- ☐ 2 cups/250 g/8 oz self-raising flour
- ☐ 2 cups/315 g/10 oz wholemeal self-raising flour
- ☐ 1 teaspoon salt
- ☐ 45 g/1¹/₂ oz butter
- ☐ 2 cups/500 mL/16 fl oz beer

1   Preheat barbecue to a medium heat. Sift together self-raising flour, wholemeal self-raising flour and salt into a bowl. Return husks to bowl. Rub in butter using fingertips until mixture resembles coarse bread crumbs. Make a well in the centre of the flour mixture and pour in beer. Using a round-bladed knife, mix to form a soft dough.

2   Turn dough onto a lightly floured surface and knead until smooth. Shape dough into a 20 cm/8 in round and place on a double thickness of oiled aluminium foil large enough to completely encase damper. Score dough into wedges using a sharp knife. Lightly dust with flour and wrap foil loosely around damper to completely enclose. Cook on barbecue, turning several times, for 1 hour or until cooked through. Serve warm, broken into pieces, with butter if desired.

White plate and jug Corso de Fiori Plants Balmain Garden Centre

STRAWBERRY AND APPLE TART

Serves 10
Oven temperature 200°C, 400°F, Gas 6

- ☐ **375 g/12 oz prepared shortcrust pastry**

STRAWBERRY FILLING
- ☐ **30 g/1 oz butter**
- ☐ **3 cooking apples, cored, peeled and chopped**
- ☐ **2 teaspoons lemon juice**
- ☐ **500 g/1 lb small strawberries, hulled**
- ☐ **2 tablespoons caster sugar**
- ☐ **1 teaspoon nutmeg**

1   To make filling, melt butter in a frying pan and cook apples with lemon juice over a high heat for 2-3 minutes or until tender. Remove from heat and add strawberries. Set aside and allow to cool completely. Stir in sugar and nutmeg.

2   Roll out two-thirds pastry to 3 mm/^{1}/8 in thickness and line a greased 23 cm/9 in fluted flan tin with removable base. Line pastry with nonstick baking paper and weigh down with uncooked rice. Bake for 10 minutes, then remove rice and paper and bake for 10-15 minutes longer or until cooked. Set aside to cool.

To serve: Spoon filling into pastry case.

Strawberry and Apple Tart

HONEY AND LAMB SKEWERS

Makes 10 kebabs

- ☐ 750 g/1¹/₂ lb lamb fillets, cut into cubes
- ☐ 1 large eggplant (aubergine), cut into cubes
- ☐ 10 bamboo skewers, lightly oiled

HONEY MARINADE
- ☐ ¹/₂ cup/125 mL/4 fl oz olive oil
- ☐ ¹/₄ cup/60 mL/2 fl oz dry sherry
- ☐ 1 clove garlic, crushed
- ☐ 2 tablespoons honey
- ☐ 1 tablespoon grated fresh ginger
- ☐ 2 tablespoons soy sauce

1 To make marinade, place oil, sherry, garlic, honey, ginger and soy sauce in a bowl and mix to combine. Add lamb and toss to coat. Cover and set aside to marinate, for at least 2 hours.

2 Place eggplant (aubergine) in a colander, sprinkle with salt and set aside for 30 minutes. Rinse under cold running water and pat dry with absorbent kitchen paper.

3 Preheat barbecue to a high heat. Thread eggplant (aubergine) and lamb, alternately, onto bamboo skewers. Reserve marinade. Cook kebabs on lightly oiled barbecue, brushing with reserved marinade and turning frequently, for 5-6 minutes or until lamb is cooked to your liking. Serve immediately.

BACON AND CHILLI SCALLOP SKEWERS

Makes 10 kebabs

- ☐ 10 thin rashers lean bacon
- ☐ 1 kg/2 lb scallops, cleaned, or 500 g firm white fish fillets, cut into 2.5 cm/1 in pieces
- ☐ 10 bamboo skewers, lightly oiled

CHILLI MARINADE
- ☐ 1 tablespoon vegetable oil
- ☐ 2 tablespoons lemon juice
- ☐ 2 teaspoons paprika
- ☐ ¹/₂ teaspoon curry powder
- ☐ pinch chilli powder
- ☐ 2 tablespoons sugar
- ☐ ¹/₂ teaspoon ground cumin
- ☐ 1 tablespoon finely chopped fresh coriander

1 To make marinade, place oil, lemon juice, paprika, curry powder, chilli powder, sugar, cumin and coriander in a bowl and mix to combine. Add scallops or fish pieces and toss to combine. Set aside to marinate for 1 hour.

2 Preheat barbecue to a high heat. Cut bacon into 7.5 cm/3 in strips and cook in a frying pan over a low heat for 4-5 minutes or until just soft. Remove and drain on absorbent kitchen paper. Wrap a piece of bacon around each scallop or fish piece and thread 4 bacon-wrapped scallops or fish pieces onto a bamboo skewer. Repeat with remaining scallops or fish pieces and skewers. Cook on lightly oiled barbecue, brushing with remaining marinade and turning frequently, for 3-4 minutes or until bacon is crisp and scallops or fish pieces are cooked.

From left: Chicken and Leek Skewers, Mushroom and Vegetable Skewers, Skewered Beef Strips, Avocado and Prawn Skewers, Honey and Lamb Skewers, Bacon and Chilli Scallop Skewers

40

- ☐ ½ cup/125 mL/4 fl oz soy sauce
- ☐ ½ cup/125 mL/4 fl oz dry sherry
- ☐ 2 teaspoons sugar

1 To make marinade, place garlic, ginger, soy sauce, sherry and sugar in a small saucepan and bring to the boil. Set aside to cool completely.

2 Place chicken and leeks in a bowl and pour marinade over. Cover and set aside to marinate for 30 minutes.

3 Preheat barbecue to a high heat. Thread chicken and leek pieces, alternately, onto bamboo skewers. Cook on lightly oiled barbecue, brushing with marinade and turning frequently, for 4-5 minutes or until chicken is cooked.

MUSHROOM AND VEGETABLE SKEWERS

Makes 8 kebabs

- ☐ 4 small red onions, halved
- ☐ 1 fennel bulb, quartered
- ☐ 1 green pepper, quartered and seeds removed
- ☐ 1 red pepper, quartered and seeds removed
- ☐ 16 button mushrooms
- ☐ 8 bamboo skewers, lightly oiled

LEMON MARINADE
- ☐ 2 tablespoons vegetable oil
- ☐ 2 tablespoons lemon juice
- ☐ 2 tablespoons finely chopped fresh parsley

1 Bring a large saucepan of water to the boil and blanch onions, fennel and green and red pepper, separately, for 2-3 minutes each. Drain vegetables and refresh under cold running water.

2 Cut each fennel quarter into four pieces and cut peppers into cubes. Thread onion halves, fennel pieces, red pepper cubes, green pepper cubes and mushrooms onto bamboo skewers. Place kebabs in a shallow glass or ceramic dish.

3 To make marinade, place oil, lemon juice and parsley in a small bowl and mix to combine. Pour marinade over kebabs in dish, cover and set aside for 1 hour. Preheat barbecue to a high heat. Drain kebabs and cook on lightly oiled barbecue, brushing with marinade and turning frequently, for 3-4 minutes or until vegetables are heated.

CHICKEN AND LEEK SKEWERS

Makes 10 kebabs

- ☐ 3 chicken breast fillets, skin removed and cut into cubes
- ☐ 4 small leeks, cut into 2.5 cm/1 in lengths
- ☐ 10 bamboo skewers, lightly oiled

GINGER MARINADE
- ☐ 1 clove garlic, crushed
- ☐ 2 teaspoons grated fresh ginger

AVOCADO AND PRAWN SKEWERS

Makes 10 kebabs

- ☐ 2 avocados, cut into cubes
- ☐ 3 tablespoons lemon juice
- ☐ 20 cooked large prawns, shelled
- ☐ 10 cherry tomatoes, halved
- ☐ 10 bamboo skewers, lightly oiled

TOMATO DIPPING SAUCE
- ☐ ½ cup/125 g/4 oz sour cream
- ☐ ½ cup/125 g/4 oz mayonnaise
- ☐ 2 tablespoons tomato sauce
- ☐ 2 teaspoons Worcestershire sauce

1 Place avocado cubes in a bowl, pour lemon juice over and toss to coat. Thread 2 prawns, 2 avocado cubes and 2 tomato halves, alternately, onto bamboo skewers.

2 To make dipping sauce, place sour cream, mayonnaise, tomato sauce and Worcestershire sauce in a bowl and mix to combine. Serve sauce with skewers for dipping.

SKEWERED BEEF STRIPS

Makes 10 kebabs

- ☐ 750 g/1½ lb blade or chuck steaks, each 3 cm/1¼ in thick
- ☐ 10 bamboo skewers, lightly oiled

RED WINE MARINADE
- ☐ 1 cup/250 mL/8 fl oz red wine
- ☐ ⅓ cup/90 mL/3 fl oz vegetable oil
- ☐ 2 bay leaves, crushed
- ☐ 2 teaspoons hot mustard
- ☐ ½ teaspoon dried thyme
- ☐ ½ teaspoon dried oregano
- ☐ freshly ground black pepper

1 Cut diagonally across each steak to make thin strips.

2 To make marinade, place wine, oil, bay leaves, mustard, thyme, oregano and black pepper to taste in a bowl and mix to combine. Add beef strips and toss to coat. Cover and marinate in the refrigerator overnight.

3 Preheat barbecue to a high heat. Remove beef from marinade and reserve marinade. Weave beef strips onto bamboo skewers and cook on lightly oiled barbecue, brushing with marinade, and turning frequently, for 3-4 minutes or until cooked.

MARINATED MUSHROOM SALAD

Serves 10

- ☐ **4 tablespoons olive oil**
- ☐ **2 cloves garlic, crushed**
- ☐ **750 g/1¹/₂ lb small button mushrooms, trimmed**
- ☐ **2 tablespoons red wine vinegar**
- ☐ **1 tablespoon lemon juice**
- ☐ **3 tablespoons chicken stock**
- ☐ **1 tablespoon chopped fresh basil**
- ☐ **2 tablespoons chopped fresh parsley**

1   Heat oil in a frying pan and cook garlic and mushrooms for 2-3 minutes. Reduce heat, add vinegar, lemon juice and stock, and simmer for 1 minute.

2   Stir in basil and parsley and set aside to cool. Cover cooled mushroom mixture and refrigerate until required.

BARBECUED CHIPS

Serves 10

- ☐ **500 g/1 lb potatoes, cut crosswise into 5 mm/¹/₄ in slices**
- ☐ **500 g/1 lb parsnips, cut lengthwise into 5 mm/¹/₄ in slices**
- ☐ **500 g/1 lb sweet potatoes, cut crosswise into 5 mm/¹/₄ in slices**
- ☐ **3 tablespoons olive oil**
- ☐ **4 onions, chopped**

1   Blanch potato, parsnip and sweet potato slices in a large saucepan of boiling water for 2 minutes. Drain, rinse under cold running water and drain on absorbent kitchen paper.

2   Preheat barbecue to a medium heat. Heat oil in a large frying pan on barbecue and cook onions for 15-20 minutes or until golden and crisp. Add potato, parsnip and sweet potato slices and cook for 10 minutes or until chips are tender.

Barbecued Chips, Marinated Mushroom Salad, Vegetable Burgers

VEGETABLE BURGERS

Makes 10 burgers

- ☐ **10 wholemeal rolls, split**
- ☐ **10 lettuce leaves**

MIXED VEGETABLE PATTIES
- ☐ **500 g/1 lb broccoli, chopped**
- ☐ **500 g/1 lb zucchini (courgettes), chopped**
- ☐ **250 g/8 oz carrots, chopped**
- ☐ **2 onions, finely chopped**
- ☐ **2 cloves garlic, crushed**
- ☐ **3 tablespoons chopped parsley**
- ☐ **3 cups/185 g/6 oz dried bread crumbs**
- ☐ **¹/₂ cup/60 g/2 oz flour, sifted**
- ☐ **freshly ground black pepper**

SPICY TOMATO SAUCE
- ☐ **1 tablespoon olive oil**
- ☐ **1 onion, finely chopped**
- ☐ **1 clove garlic, crushed**
- ☐ **1 fresh red chilli, seeded and finely chopped**
- ☐ **1 green pepper, finely chopped**
- ☐ **440 g/14 oz canned tomatoes, undrained and mashed**
- ☐ **freshly ground black pepper**

1 To make patties, boil, steam or microwave broccoli, zucchini (courgettes) and carrots until tender. Drain, rinse under cold running water and pat dry.

2 Place broccoli, zucchini (courgettes), carrots, onions, garlic and parsley in a food processor and process until puréed. Transfer vegetable mixture to a mixing bowl, add bread crumbs and flour, season with black pepper and mix to combine. Cover and refrigerate for 30 minutes.

3 Shape mixture into ten patties. Place on a tray lined with nonstick baking paper, cover and refrigerate until required.

4 To make sauce, heat oil in a saucepan and cook onion, garlic, chilli and green pepper for 5 minutes or until onion and green pepper are soft. Add tomatoes, bring mixture to the boil, then reduce heat and simmer for 15-20 minutes or until sauce thickens. Season to taste with black pepper.

5 Preheat barbecue to a medium heat. Cook patties on lightly oiled barbecue plate (griddle) or in a lightly oiled frying pan on barbecue for 3-4 minutes each side. Toast rolls on barbecue. Place a lettuce leaf, a pattie, and a spoonful of sauce on the bottom half of each roll, top with remaining roll half and serve immediately.

Menus for Summer Days

SEAFOOD BARBECUE FOR SIX

Hot Chilli Prawns
(page 63)

Grilled Trout with Apple Stuffing
(Make 1½ quantity of this recipe)
(page 60)

Savoury Bread
(page 58)

Barbecued Potato Skins
(page 65)

Blue Cheese Caesar Salad
(Make ½ quantity of this recipe)
(page 38)

Mixed Lettuce and Herb Salad

Strawberry and Apple Tart
(page 39)

VEGETARIAN BARBECUE FOR SIX

Mushroom and Vegetable Skewers
(Make 1½ quantity of this recipe –
this allows 2 skewers per person)
(page 41)

Vegetable Burgers
(Make ½ the recipe of burgers – this
will be enough to make six patties.
Make ½ recipe of sauce. You will
only need 6 rolls and 6 lettuce leaves)
(page 43)

Green Lettuce Salad

Potato Salad

Brown Ale Damper
(page 38)

Fresh Fruit

IMPROMPTU FAMILY BARBECUE FOR SIX

Lamb Cutlets with
Honey Butter
(Make 1½ quantity of this recipe)
(page 67)

Char-grilled Vegetable Slices
(page 54)

Garlic Baked Potatoes
(page 50)

Savoury Bread
(page 58)

Fruit and Cheese Platter
(Make ½ quantity of this recipe)
(page 16)

MEAT LOVERS BARBECUE FOR SIX

Mixed Satays
(page 23)

Barbecued Steak Sandwiches
(page 57)

Barbecued Chips
(page 42)

Salad Bar
(page 9)

Marshmallow Surprises
(page 10)

A BIRTHDAY BARBECUE
FOR TEN

Pitta Crisps
(page 8)

Guacamole with Tortillas
(page 32)

Hot Chilli Pork Spareribs
(page 32)

Mixed Sausage and Onion Grill
Allow 20 sausages, 5 onions and 20
baby new potatoes)
(page 54)

Chicken with Creamy Pesto Stuffing
(page 38)

Lettuce, Avocado and Tomato Salad

Potato Salad

Savoury Bread
(page 58)

Birthday Cake

COUNTDOWN FOR BIRTHDAY BARBECUE

Use this countdown to ensure that your birthday barbecue runs to plan.

SEVERAL WEEKS IN ADVANCE
✧ Draw up your guest list and invite your guests.

SEVERAL DAYS IN ADVANCE
✧ Check that everyone has replied to their invitations and you know how many people are coming to the party.
✧ Check the barbecue area and seating arrangements. Organise extra chairs if you need to – borrow from friends or hire.
✧ Decide whether you are going to make or buy the birthday cake. If you are going to buy it, order it to ensure that you get the one you want. If you are going to make it, decide on your recipe and check that you have all the ingredients.
✧ Check that your barbecue is working and clean.
✧ If you have a gas barbecue get the gas bottle filled.
✧ If your barbecue requires coals or wood check that you have enough fuel.
✧ Make two shopping lists, one for perishable and one for nonperishable items.
✧ Purchase nonperishable items – don't forget paper napkins and plates if you are going to use them.

THE DAY BEFORE
✧ Purchase perishable items.
✧ Make birthday cake if you are making it yourself. Store in an airtight container.
✧ Make Pitta Crisps and store in an airtight container.
✧ Prepare Savoury Bread and store in the refrigerator.
✧ Make Chilli Butter for Guacamole and Tortillas with Chilli Butter. Store, covered, in the refrigerator.
✧ Make glaze and marinade for ribs. Store in a screwtop jar in the refrigerator.
✧ Cook potatoes for potato salad and Mixed Sausage and Onion Grill. Cool and store, covered, in the refrigerator.
✧ Make up dressings for salads. Store in screwtop jars in the refrigerator.
✧ Make Creamy Pesto Stuffing for chicken. Store, covered, in refrigerator.

EARLIER IN DAY
✧ Arrange barbecue area and set table.
✧ Decorate birthday cake. Remember, if you have used fresh cream store cake in the refrigerator
✧ Place ribs into marinade.
✧ Prepare chicken and store in refrigerator until just prior to cooking.
✧ Prepare salads but do not add dressing.
✧ Place onions and potatoes on skewers for Mixed Sausage and Onion Grill.

ONE AND HALF HOURS BEFORE EATING
✧ Wood or coal barbecues usually take at least an hour to heat up, so allow sufficient time so that your barbecue is hot when you are ready to cook.
✧ Make Guacamole and assemble Guacamole and Tortillas platter.
✧ Place Pitta Crisps in basket or on plate.

35 MINUTES BEFORE EATING
✧ If you have a gas barbecue, light it 5-10 minutes before you want to start cooking – or according to the manufacturer's instructions.
✧ Place chicken on to cook.

20 MINUTES AND UP TO EATING
✧ Place onions for Mixed Sausage and Onion Grill on to cook.
✧ Place ribs on to cook.
✧ Place bread on to reheat.
✧ Reheat glaze for ribs.
✧ Dress salads.

BARBECUE BASICS

A barbecue is often an impromptu affair. In this section you will find easy ideas and recipes for making that piece of steak or those lamb chops into something special.

In the Barbecue Secrets chapter you will find sauces and marinades, plus information on equipment, safety, techniques and different types of barbecues – all the little extras that will ensure that your barbecue cooking is the best in the street.

The word barbecue comes from the American Spanish word 'barbacoa'. In the seventeenth century shipwrecked sailors and runaway slaves took refuge on the island of Hispaniola in the Caribbean where they discovered the Indians' method of smoke-

Barbecue tools Bibelot, *Skewers, sauceboat, salt and pepper mill* The Bay Tree

drying meat over hot coals on wood grids. The Spanish, impressed by this type of cooking, took it to Mexico and the American Southwest where it soon became popular. By the late 1880s, cattle ranchers in America had found that cooking ribs and large pieces of meat on metal grids over hot coals was the ideal way to feed hungry cowboys.

Around the world, barbecues are used for entertaining and fund-raising. In America, Texas-style ribs, clambakes and spit-roasted pig are popular ways of feeding large crowds at fairs and political rallies. In Australia, barbecues are set up at many sports gatherings, where steak and sausage sandwiches are the main fare.

Dishes from many countries make great barbecue food. The kebabs of Asian and Middle Eastern cuisines are ideal for barbecuing. Remember that stir-fries can be cooked in a wok or frying pan on the barbecue and there are some wonderful Indian recipes for marinades and sauces that will add sensational flavours to lamb, beef, poultry and seafood.

No matter whether your barbecue is a grand occasion or simply a family get-together, read on and find the recipes, hints and tips to make it a huge success.

Sizzling Sensations

Beef and lamb are without doubt the most popular barbecue fare, however there are many alternatives that are equally delicious. Why not try Vegetable Kebabs with Creamy Mustard Sauce for something different?

*Curried Chicken Kebabs,
Seafood Kebabs,
Garlic Baked Potatoes
(recipes page 50)*

CURRIED CHICKEN KEBABS

Serves 6

- [ ] **750 g/1¹/₂ lb chicken breast fillets, skin removed, cut into 2.5 cm/1 in cubes**
- [ ] **12 skewers, lightly oiled**

LIME CURRY GLAZE
- [ ] **1 cup/315 g/10 oz lime marmalade**
- [ ] **2 tablespoons Dijon mustard**
- [ ] **2 teaspoons curry powder**
- [ ] **1 tablespoon lime juice**

1 To make glaze, place marmalade, mustard, curry powder and lime juice in a small saucepan and cook, stirring, over a medium heat for 3 minutes or until ingredients are combined. Remove from heat and set aside to cool.

2 Thread chicken cubes onto skewers. Place skewers in a shallow glass or ceramic dish, spoon glaze over, cover and set aside to marinate at room temperature for 1 hour.

3 Preheat barbecue to a medium heat. Remove chicken from glaze and reserve any remaining glaze. Cook kebabs on lightly oiled barbecue, brushing kebabs with reserved glaze and turning frequently, for 8-10 minutes or until cooked.

SEAFOOD KEBABS

Serves 4

- [ ] **8 skewers, lightly oiled**
- [ ] **8 large uncooked prawns, peeled and deveined with tails left intact**
- [ ] **8 scallops**
- [ ] **1 large white fish fillet, cut into 8 x 2 cm/³/₄ in cubes**
- [ ] **1 salmon fillet, cut into 8 x 2 cm/³/₄ in cubes**
- [ ] **8 mussels, removed from shells**

CHILLI LIME GLAZE
- [ ] **¹/₄ cup/60 mL/2 fl oz olive oil**
- [ ] **2 fresh red chillies, seeds removed and finely chopped**
- [ ] **1 clove garlic, crushed**
- [ ] **¹/₄ cup/60 mL/2 fl oz lime juice**

1 Preheat barbecue to a medium heat. Alternately thread a mussel, a piece of white fish, a prawn, a scallop and a piece of salmon onto a skewer. Repeat with remaining seafood and skewers.

2 To make glaze, place oil, chillies, garlic and lime juice in a small bowl and mix to combine. Brush kebabs with glaze and cook on lightly oiled barbecue, turning frequently and brushing with remaining glaze, until seafood changes colour and is cooked through. Serve immediately.

GARLIC BAKED POTATOES

Delicately flavoured Garlic Baked Potatoes are the perfect accompaniment to any barbecue.

Serves 6

- [ ] **6 large potatoes, scrubbed**
- [ ] **3 teaspoons olive oil**
- [ ] **1 tablespoon finely chopped fresh rosemary**
- [ ] **freshly ground black pepper**
- [ ] **6 cloves garlic, peeled and cut in half**

1 Preheat barbecue to a medium heat. Using an apple corer, carefully remove a plug from each potato, making sure not to go right through the potato. Reserve the plugs.

2 Combine oil, rosemary and black pepper. Fill hole in each potato with two garlic halves and a little oil mixture. Cut off two-thirds of each plug and discard. Replace remaining plug in potato and wrap potatoes in aluminium foil. Cook potatoes on barbecue for 1 hour or until tender.

Salmon Cutlets with Pineapple Salsa

SALMON CUTLETS
WITH PINEAPPLE SALSA

*This salsa is delicious served with
any fish or barbecued chicken.*

Serves 4

- ☐ **4 salmon cutlets, cut 2.5 cm/1 in
  thick**

PINEAPPLE SALSA
- ☐ **250 g/8 oz roughly chopped fresh
  pineapple**
- ☐ **2 spring onions, finely chopped**
- ☐ **1 fresh red chilli, seeded and
  finely chopped**
- ☐ **1 tablespoon lemon juice**
- ☐ **2 tablespoons finely chopped
  fresh mint**

1   Preheat barbecue to a medium heat.
Cook salmon cutlets on lightly oiled
barbecue for 3-5 minutes each side or until
flesh flakes when tested with a fork.

2   To make salsa, place pineapple, spring
onions, chilli, lemon juice and mint in a
food processor or blender and process
to combine. Serve at room temperature
with salmon cutlets.

Cook's tip: If fresh pineapple is unavailable
use a can of drained crushed pineapple in
natural juice in its place.

Variation: Salmon cutlets are also delicious
served with Lemon or Lime Butter (see
page 70 for making flavoured butters).

Sizzling Shortcuts

Lamb and beef are all-time barbecue favourites.
The barbecue gives the meat a delicious smoky flavour
and the quick, dry heat seals the outside of the meat,
keeping the inside tender and juicy.

CHEESE-FILLED BEEF PATTIES

Serves 4

- ☐ **600 g/1¼ lb lean minced beef**
- ☐ **1 tablespoon barbecue sauce**
- ☐ **2 tablespoons tomato sauce**
- ☐ **1 small onion, finely chopped**
- ☐ **60 g/2 oz grated tasty cheese (mature Cheddar)**
- ☐ **125 g/4 oz canned crushed pineapple, drained**

1   Preheat barbecue to a medium heat. Place beef, barbecue sauce, tomato sauce and onion in a bowl and mix to combine. Shape beef mixture into eight patties.

2   Top 4 patties with cheese and pineapple, then cover with remaining patties, carefully moulding edges of patties together.

3   Cook patties on lightly oiled barbecue for 4-5 minutes each side.

CHILLI LAMB SATAY

Serves 6

- ☐ **750 g/1½ lb lamb leg steaks, all visible fat removed, cut into cubes**

CHILLI MARINADE
- ☐ **1 onion, roughly chopped**
- ☐ **2 cloves garlic, crushed**
- ☐ **1 fresh red chilli, seeded and chopped**
- ☐ **2 tablespoons desiccated coconut**
- ☐ **3 tablespoons lemon juice**
- ☐ **1 tablespoon soy sauce**

SATAY SAUCE
- ☐ **¹/₂ cup/125 g/4 oz peanut butter**
- ☐ **¹/₂ cup/125 mL/4 fl oz hot water**
- ☐ **¹/₄ teaspoon chilli sauce**
- ☐ **1 tablespoon lemon juice**
- ☐ **1 tablespoon soy sauce**

1   To make marinade, place onion, garlic, chilli, coconut, lemon juice and soy sauce in a food processor or blender and process to combine.

2   Place lamb in a shallow glass or ceramic dish and pour marinade over. Cover and set aside to marinate for at least 30 minutes. Drain lamb and thread onto oiled skewers. Preheat barbecue to a medium heat. Cook kebabs on lightly oiled barbecue, turning occasionally, for 8-10 minutes or until cooked to your liking.

3   To make sauce, place peanut butter, water and chilli sauce in a small saucepan and cook, stirring, over a medium heat until combined and heated through. Remove pan from heat and stir in lemon juice and soy sauce. Serve sauce with kebabs.

From left: Cheese-Filled Beef Patties, Chilli Lamb Satay, Ginger and Pineapple Lamb Cutlets

GINGER AND PINEAPPLE LAMB CUTLETS

Serves 4

- ☐ 8 lean lamb cutlets, trimmed of all visible fat
- ☐ 440 g/14 oz canned pineapple slices, in natural juice, drained and juice reserved

GINGER GLAZE
- ☐ 1 tablespoon reserved pineapple juice
- ☐ 2 tablespoons marmalade
- ☐ 1/2 teaspoon ground ginger

1 Preheat barbecue to a medium heat. To make glaze, place pineapple juice, marmalade and ginger in a small bowl and mix to combine.

2 Brush cutlets with glaze. Cook cutlets on lightly oiled barbecue, brushing frequently with glaze, for 3-4 minutes each side or until cooked to your liking. Cook pineapple on barbecue for 2-3 minutes each side or until brown. Serve pineapple with cutlets.

COOKING THE PERFECT STEAK

These instructions will ensure that you always cook the perfect steak on the barbecue. The secret is to retain as much of the meat's natural juices as possible.

☐ T-bone, sirloin, rump, fillet or rib eye steaks, trim of all visible fat

1 Preheat barbecue to hot.
2 Sear steaks for 2-3 minutes each side. After searing, reduce the heat of the barbecue or move steaks to a cooler section of the barbecue.
3 Cook to your liking, using the chart as a guide to cooking times.
4 Do not turn steak too often – twice during the entire cooking should be enough. When turning the steak use tongs. Do not use a fork as this pierces the surface and juices will escape causing the meat to become dry and tough.
5 When testing to see if a steak is cooked to your liking, press it with a pair of blunt tongs. Do not cut the meat as this causes the juices to escape. Rare steaks will feel springy to the touch, medium steaks slightly springy and well-done steaks will feel firm.
6 When cooking for a crowd, ask your butcher to cut the steaks to different thicknesses. This means that you can cook them all at the one time; the thinner steaks will be well done and the thicker steaks rare.

COOKING TIMES FOR STEAKS

Thickness of steak	Cooking time each side in minutes		
	Rare	Medium	Well-done
2.5 cm/1 in	3	4	5
5 cm/2 in	4	5	7

MIXED SAUSAGE
AND ONION GRILL

Buy a selection of your favourite sausages for this mixed grill. Mild or hot Italian sausages, bratwurst, knackwurst, pork, beef, or some of the more exotic flavours such as lamb and mint or turkey and sage are all delicious choices.

Serves 6

- [ ] **12 sausages of different varieties**
- [ ] **12 baby new potatoes, scrubbed**
- [ ] **3 red onions, cut into quarters**
- [ ] **12 skewers, lightly oiled**
- [ ] **olive oil**

1   Parboil sausages (see Barbecue a Sausage). Drain and set aside to cool, then refrigerate.

2   Boil, steam or microwave potatoes until just tender.

3   Preheat barbecue to a medium heat. Thread 2 onion quarters onto 6 of the skewers, then brush with oil. Cook on lightly oiled barbecue, turning halfway through cooking, for 15-20 minutes or until onions are golden and tender.

4   Thread 2 potatoes onto each of the remaining skewers, then brush with oil. Cook on barbecue, turning halfway through cooking, for 10-15 minutes or until potatoes are golden and heated through.

5   Cook sausages on lightly oiled barbecue for 10-15 minutes or until sausages are golden and crisp on the outside and heated through.

Serving suggestion: Serve with a selection of mustards and sauces.

CHAR-GRILLED
VEGETABLE SLICES

Serves 6

- [ ] **½ cup/125 mL/4 fl oz olive oil**
- [ ] **1 clove garlic, crushed**
- [ ] **1 large eggplant (aubergine), cut lengthwise into thick slices**
- [ ] **3 large zucchini (courgettes), cut lengthwise into thick slices**
- [ ] **2 red peppers, cut into quarters, seeds removed**
- [ ] **3 large firm tomatoes, cut into thick slices**
- [ ] **freshly ground black pepper**

1   Preheat barbecue to a medium heat. Place oil and garlic in a small bowl and whisk to combine. Brush eggplant (aubergine) slices, zucchini (courgette) slices, red pepper slices and tomato slices with oil mixture.

2   Cook eggplant (aubergine), zucchini (courgette) and red pepper slices on lightly oiled barbecue, turning frequently, for 4-5 minutes or until almost cooked. Add tomato slices to barbecue and cook all vegetables for 2-3 minutes longer.

*Mixed Sausage and Onion Grill,
Char-grilled Vegetable Slices*

Plants Balmain Garden Centre

BARBECUE A SAUSAGE

Children and adults alike love sausages cooked on the barbecue. With the huge variety now available from butchers, specialty shops and delicatessens, you have no fear of sausages ever being dull.

To cook the perfect barbecued sausage it should be parboiled first. This ensures that the sausage will be cooked on the inside and golden on the outside and will remove some of the fat in it.

To parboil, place sausages in a saucepan, cover with water and bring slowly to the boil, then reduce heat and simmer for 5 minutes. Drain and set aside to cool. When cool, cover and refrigerate for several hours or overnight. Preheat barbecue to a medium heat. Cook sausages on lightly oiled barbecue, turning several times, for 10 minutes or until golden and heated through.

BARBECUED STEAK SANDWICHES

Marinated steak, barbecued and placed between slices of grilled bread makes the best steak sandwiches you will ever taste.

Serves 6

- ☐ **6 lean rump steaks, cut 1 cm/¹/₂ in thick**
- ☐ **3 onions, finely sliced**
- ☐ **12 thick slices wholemeal or grain bread**
- ☐ **olive oil**

GINGER WINE MARINADE
- ☐ **1 cup/250 mL/8 fl oz red wine**
- ☐ **¹/₂ cup/125 mL/4 fl oz olive oil**
- ☐ **1 clove garlic, crushed**
- ☐ **2 teaspoons grated fresh ginger**

1 To make marinade, place wine, oil, garlic and ginger in a bowl and mix to combine. Place steaks in a shallow glass or ceramic dish. Pour marinade over, cover, and marinate at room temperature for 2-3 hours or overnight in the refrigerator.

2 Cook onions on lightly oiled barbecue plate (griddle) or in a lightly oiled frying pan on barbecue for 10-15 minutes or until golden. Preheat barbecue to a medium heat. Drain steaks and cook on lightly oiled barbecue for 3-5 minutes each side or until cooked to your liking.

3 Lightly brush bread slices with oil and cook on barbecue grill for 1-2 minutes each side or until lightly toasted. To assemble sandwiches, top 6 toasted bread slices with steak, onions and remaining bread slices.

Cook's tip: You may like to add some salad ingredients to your sandwiches. Mustard or relish is also a tasty addition.

Left: Barbecued Steak Sandwiches
Above: Caribbean Spatchcock

CARIBBEAN SPATCHCOCK

Serves 6

- ☐ **3 spatchcocks (poussins), halved**
- ☐ **2 tablespoons cracked black pepper**
- ☐ **1 teaspoon ground coriander**

LIME MARINADE
- ☐ **3 tablespoons white rum**
- ☐ **2 teaspoons finely grated lime rind**
- ☐ **1 tablespoon lime juice**
- ☐ **2 tablespoons honey**
- ☐ **2 cloves garlic, crushed**
- ☐ **1 teaspoon grated fresh ginger**

1 To make marinade, place rum, lime rind, lime juice, honey, garlic and ginger in a bowl and mix to combine. Place spatchcock (poussin) halves in a shallow glass or ceramic dish and rub marinade into spatchcocks (poussins). Cover and set aside to marinate for 1 hour.

2 Preheat barbecue to a medium heat. Thread a skewer through wings and legs of each spatchcock (poussin) half and brush with any remaining marinade. Combine black pepper and coriander and press onto skin of birds. Cook on lightly oiled barbecue grill, turning frequently for 15-20 minutes or until birds are cooked through.

Cook's tip: This is also a delicious way to prepare and cook chicken pieces. Instead of using spatchcocks, simply use chicken pieces and prepare and marinate as in this recipe – the cooking time for the chicken pieces will be about the same as for the spatchcocks. You should cook them until the juices run clear.

SAVOURY BREAD

Garlic and herb breads are easy to make and can be prepared in advance and frozen if you wish.

Serves 8

☐ **1 large French stick**

FLAVOURED BUTTER
☐ **125 g/4 oz butter, softened**
☐ **2 cloves garlic, crushed; or 2 tablespoons finely chopped fresh herbs – choose from rosemary, parsley, thyme, chives**
☐ **freshly ground black pepper**

1   Preheat barbecue to a medium heat. Slice bread on a slight diagonal, at 2 cm/³/₄ in intervals almost all the way through so that the slices remain joined at the base.

2   To make Flavoured Butter, place butter, garlic or herbs and black pepper to taste in a food processor and process to combine.

3   Spread one side of each slice of bread with Flavoured Butter. Wrap loaf in a double thickness of aluminium foil and heat on barbecue for 15-20 minutes or until bread is heated.

FOIL-WRAPPED CHICKEN BREASTS

Serves 6

☐ **6 chicken breast fillets, skin removed and pounded**
☐ **60 g/2 oz butter**
☐ **1 small onion, chopped**
☐ **1 clove garlic, crushed**
☐ **2 cups/125 g/4 oz bread crumbs, made from stale bread**
☐ **3 tablespoons finely chopped fresh parsley**
☐ **freshly ground black pepper**

1   Preheat barbecue to a medium heat. Melt 15 g/¹/₂ oz butter in a small frying pan and cook onion and garlic over a medium heat for 3-4 minutes or until onion is soft.

2   Place bread crumbs in a bowl, add onion mixture and parsley. Melt remaining butter and mix into bread crumb mixture. Season to taste with black pepper.

3   Cut six pieces of heavy-duty aluminium foil large enough to enclose chicken breast fillets. Brush foil lightly with oil and place a fillet on each piece of foil. Top one half of each fillet with some stuffing and fold fillet over to enclose. Wrap foil around chicken to form a tight parcel so that juices will not escape during cooking.

4   Place foil parcels on barbecue and cook, turning halfway through cooking, for 10-15 minutes or until chicken is cooked and tender.

Cook's tip: If you do not have heavy-duty aluminium foil, use a double thickness of ordinary foil instead.

Butterfly
a Leg

Boning a leg of lamb yourself is not nearly as daunting as you may think, as long as you remember that a sharp knife is essential and that the knife should always stay as close as possible to the bone.

1 Turn the leg of lamb so that the skin side is lying flat on your work surface and the thick end of the leg is facing you. Using a sharp knife, cut around the edges of the pelvic bone at the thick end (the pelvic bone is the one that you can see). This will loosen the bone.

2 Now cut deep around the pelvic bone, until you have freed it at the joint and through the tendons that connect it to the leg bone (the leg bone is the middle bone in the joint). Remember to keep your knife as close as possible to the bone so that you do not cut into the meat.

3 The next step is to remove the shank bone. Hold on to this bone at the tip and cut close to the bone to free tendons and meat. Continue cutting down the bone until you reach the joint that connects it to the leg bone, cut through the tendons at this joint and remove the shank bone.

4 The leg bone is now removed in a tunnel fashion by gently loosening the meat at either end of the bone then cutting the meat from the bone and easing it out as you work. The leg of lamb is now boned and all you have to do is to butterfly it. This is done by placing your knife horizontally in the cavity left by the leg bone and partially splitting the meat open. The flap is then turned outwards and the meat spread flat. Now make a similar horizontal cut into the thick muscle opposite so that it too can be opened out flat.

MARINATED
LEG OF LAMB

Your butcher will butterfly the leg in minutes for you, or you can do it yourself.

Serves 6

- ☐ **1.5-2 kg/3-4 lb leg of lamb, butterflied**
- ☐ **freshly ground black pepper**

LEMON HERB MARINADE
- ☐ **2 cloves garlic, crushed**
- ☐ **1/4 cup/60 mL/ 2 fl oz olive oil**
- ☐ **1/4 cup/60 mL/2 fl oz lemon juice**
- ☐ **1 tablespoon finely chopped fresh marjoram or 1 teaspoon dried marjoram**
- ☐ **1 tablespoon finely chopped fresh thyme or 1 teaspoon dried thyme**

1 Lay lamb out flat and season well with black pepper. Place in a shallow glass or ceramic dish.

2 To make marinade, place garlic, oil, lemon juice, marjoram and thyme in a small bowl and mix to combine. Pour marinade over lamb, cover and allow to marinate at room temperature for 3-4 hours, or overnight in the refrigerator.

3 Preheat barbecue to a medium heat. Remove lamb from marinade and reserve marinade. Cook lamb on lightly oiled barbecue grill, turning several times during cooking and basting with reserved marinade, for 15-25 minutes or until cooked to your liking.

Cook's tip: Try lemon thyme instead of ordinary thyme in this recipe.

Left: Foil-wrapped Chicken Breasts, Savoury Bread
Above: Marinated Leg of Lamb

Keeping it Safe

The casual style of barbecuing can sometimes lead to casual handling of food which in turn can lead to unwelcome health problems. Follow these easy rules for safe entertaining.

PREPARATION

✧ Do not handle cooked and uncooked meat at the same time. This encourages the transfer of bacteria from raw meat to cooked meat.

✧ Wash thoroughly in hot soapy water utensils and boards that have been used for cutting raw meat, before using to cut cooked meat.

✧ Remember to thoroughly wash your hands after preparing raw meat.

STORAGE

✧ Storing raw meat, poultry or fish above or in direct contact with cooked foods can lead to the raw food dripping liquid or passing bacteria to the cooked food.

✧ Meat, fish and poultry that has been prepared in advance must be kept chilled until just prior to cooking.

✧ When entertaining make sure that you have plenty of room in your refrigerator to keep food well chilled.

✧ Remember beer and beverages can always be chilled in a tub of ice.

✧ Store cold food at temperatures below 4°C/39°F and hot food at temperatures above 60°C/140°F. Foods held at temperatures between these two are more likely to develop bacteria which can cause food poisoning.

✧ It is best to serve barbecued food immediately that it is cooked, and always on a clean plate.

GRILLED TROUT WITH APPLE STUFFING

Serves 4

- ☐ **4 small trout, cleaned, with head and tail intact**
- ☐ **olive oil**

APPLE STUFFING
- ☐ **30 g/1 oz butter**
- ☐ **1 small onion, finely chopped**
- ☐ **1 apple, cored and finely chopped**
- ☐ **1/2 cup/30 g/1 oz bread crumbs made from stale bread**
- ☐ **1 teaspoon lemon juice**
- ☐ **1 tablespoon finely chopped fresh mint**
- ☐ **2 teaspoons finely chopped parsley**
- ☐ **freshly ground black pepper**

1 Preheat barbecue to a medium heat. To make stuffing, melt butter in a frying pan and cook onion for 5 minutes or until transparent. Place apple and bread crumbs in a bowl, add onion mixture, lemon juice, mint and parsley and season to taste with black pepper. Mix to combine.

2 Fill the cavity of each trout with stuffing. Secure opening using toothpicks and lightly brush outside of each trout with oil. Cook on lightly oiled barbecue for 5-8 minutes each side or until flesh flakes when tested with a fork.

POTATO ROUNDS

Serves 4

- ☐ **4 potatoes, peeled and thinly sliced**
- ☐ **60 g/2 oz butter, melted**
- ☐ **1 teaspoon paprika**
- ☐ **1 clove garlic, crushed**
- ☐ **1 teaspoon dried mixed herbs**

1 Preheat barbecue to a medium heat. Place potatoes on absorbent kitchen paper and dry well. Combine butter, paprika, garlic and mixed herbs in a small bowl.

2 Place potato rounds in a bowl and toss with butter mixture. Cook on lightly oiled barbecue plate (griddle) brushing with remaining butter mixture and turning for 8-10 minutes or until potatoes are golden brown and tender.

BRUSCHETTA WITH TOMATO AND OLIVES

Bruschetta is the garlic bread of Italy. Delicious cooked on the barbecue, it can be eaten plain or topped with fresh tomatoes or roasted red pepper.

Serves 4

- ☐ **1/4 cup/60 mL/2 fl oz olive oil**
- ☐ **2 cloves garlic, crushed**
- ☐ **8 thick slices of crusty bread**

TOMATO OLIVE TOPPING
- ☐ **3 large ripe tomatoes, peeled and diced**
- ☐ **2 tablespoons finely chopped red pepper**
- ☐ **6 black olives, finely chopped**
- ☐ **1/2 red onion, finely chopped**
- ☐ **2 tablespoons finely chopped fresh basil**
- ☐ **1 tablespoon olive oil**
- ☐ **1 tablespoon balsamic or red wine vinegar**
- ☐ **freshly ground black pepper**

1 To make topping, place tomatoes, red pepper, olives, onion, basil, oil and vinegar in bowl, season to taste with black pepper and toss to combine.

2 Preheat barbecue to a medium heat. Combine oil and garlic and brush both sides of each slice of bread. Cook bread on lightly oiled barbecue for 2-3 minutes each side or until toasted. Serve immediately, topped with Tomato Olive Topping.

Grilled Trout with Apple Stuffing, Potato Rounds, Bruschetta with Tomatoes and Olives

SPICY FISH STICKS

Serves 4

- ☐ **4 small white fish fillets**
- ☐ **1 long French bread stick, cut into 4 lengths**
- ☐ **30g/1 oz butter**
- ☐ **1 mignonette (lollo rosso) lettuce, shredded**
- ☐ **1 tomato, sliced**
- ☐ **4 tablespoons tartare sauce**

CORIANDER AND LEMON MARINADE
- ☐ **1 tablespoon oil**
- ☐ **2 tablespoons finely chopped fresh coriander**
- ☐ **2 tablespoons fresh lemon juice**
- ☐ **¹/₄ teaspoon chilli powder**
- ☐ **¹/₂ teaspoon ground cumin**

1   To make marinade, place oil, coriander, lemon juice, chilli powder and cumin in a bowl and mix to combine. Place fish in a shallow glass or ceramic dish and pour marinade over. Cover and set aside to marinate for 15 minutes, turning once.

2   Preheat barbecue to a medium heat. Cut each piece of bread stick in half horizontally and toast on barbecue. Spread with butter, then top bottom halves of bread stick with lettuce and tomato.

3   Place fish fillets on lightly oiled barbecue plate (griddle) and cook for 2 minutes each side or until fish flakes when tested with a fork.

4   Top tomato with fish fillets, tartare sauce and remaining bread stick pieces.

Serving suggestion: These sticks are delicious served with Barbecue Potato Rounds (page 60).

VEGETABLE KEBABS WITH MUSTARD SAUCE

The baby eggplant (aubergines) can be replaced with 1 large eggplant (aubergine) cut into large pieces.

Serves 6

- ☐ **12 baby squash or 3 zucchini (courgettes), cut into chunks**
- ☐ **6 baby eggplant (aubergines), cut into chunks**
- ☐ **12 small onions, peeled**
- ☐ **12 firm cherry tomatoes**
- ☐ **12 button mushrooms**
- ☐ **12 skewers, lightly oiled**

CREAMY MUSTARD SAUCE
- ☐ **15 g/¹/₂ oz butter**
- ☐ **6 spring onions, finely chopped**
- ☐ **2 tablespoons wholegrain mustard**
- ☐ **300 g/9¹/₂ oz sour cream**
- ☐ **¹/₂ teaspoon ground cumin**

1   Preheat barbecue to a medium heat. Blanch squash or zucchini (courgettes), eggplant (aubergines) and onions for a few minutes in boiling water or in the microwave oven. Refresh under cold running water. Thread squash or zucchini (courgettes), eggplant (aubergines), onions, tomatoes and mushrooms, alternately, onto skewers. Cook on lightly oiled barbecue, turning frequently, for 5 minutes or until vegetables are golden and tender.

2   To make sauce, melt butter in a small saucepan and cook spring onions over a medium heat for 1-2 minutes or until soft. Stir in mustard, sour cream and cumin and cook over a low heat for 1 minute or until sauce is heated through. Do not allow sauce to boil or it will curdle. Spoon sauce over kebabs and serve immediately.

Left: Spicy Fish Sticks, Vegetable Kebabs with Mustard Sauce
Right: Hot Chilli Prawns

HOT CHILLI PRAWNS

Serves 6

- ☐ **1.5 kg/3 lb uncooked large prawns, peeled and deveined with tails left intact**

CHILLI MARINADE
- ☐ **2 teaspoons cracked black pepper**
- ☐ **2 tablespoons sweet chilli sauce**
- ☐ **1 tablespoon soy sauce**
- ☐ **1 clove garlic, crushed**
- ☐ **¹/₄ cup/60 mL/2 fl oz lemon juice**

MANGO CREAM
- ☐ **1 mango, peeled, stoned and roughly chopped**
- ☐ **3 tablespoons coconut milk**

1   To make marinade, place black pepper, chilli sauce, soy sauce, garlic and lemon juice in a bowl and mix to combine. Add prawns, toss to coat, cover and set aside to marinate for 1 hour. Toss several times during marinating.

2   To make Mango Cream, place mango flesh and coconut milk in a food processor or blender and process until smooth.

3   Preheat barbecue to a medium heat. Drain prawns and cook on lightly oiled barbecue for 3-4 minutes or until prawns change colour. Serve immediately with Mango Cream.

Coconut milk: This can be purchased in a number of forms: canned, as a long-life product in cartons, or as a powder to which you add water. Once opened it has a short life and should be used within a day or so. It is available from Asian food stores and some supermarkets, however if you have trouble finding it you can easily make your own. To make coconut milk, place 500 g/1 lb desiccated coconut in a bowl and add 3 cups/750 mL/1¹/₄ pt of boiling water. Set aside to stand for 30 minutes, then strain, squeezing the coconut to extract as much liquid as possible. This will make a thick coconut milk. The coconut can be used again to make a weaker coconut milk.

Plate and bowl Villa Italiana Tiles Fred Pazotti

HONEY AND SAGE PORK CHOPS

Serves 6

- ☐ **6 pork chops**

HONEY SAGE MARINADE
- ☐ **1 cup/250 mL/8 fl oz dry white wine**
- ☐ **$^1/_2$ cup/170 g/5$^1/_2$ oz honey**
- ☐ **1 tablespoon finely chopped fresh sage or 1 teaspoon dried sage**

1   To make marinade, place wine, honey and sage in a small bowl and mix to combine. Place chops in a shallow glass or ceramic dish and pour marinade over. Cover and marinate at room temperature for 2-3 hours, or overnight in the refrigerator.

2   Preheat barbecue to a medium heat. Drain chops and cook on lightly oiled barbecue for 5-6 minutes each side or until cooked.

ORIENTAL PORK FILLETS

Serves 8

- ☐ **1 kg/2 lb pork fillets**

ORIENTAL MARINADE
- ☐ **$^1/_3$ cup/90 mL/3 fl oz hoisin sauce**
- ☐ **$^1/_3$ cup/90 mL/3 fl oz tomato sauce**
- ☐ **2 tablespoons soy sauce**
- ☐ **4 tablespoons honey**
- ☐ **2 cloves garlic, crushed**
- ☐ **2 teaspoons grated fresh ginger**
- ☐ **1 teaspoon sweet chilli sauce**
- ☐ **1 teaspoon five spice powder**

1   To make marinade, place hoisin sauce, tomato sauce, soy sauce, honey, garlic, ginger, chilli sauce and five spice powder in a small bowl and mix to combine. Place fillets in a shallow glass or ceramic dish and pour marinade over. Cover and refrigerate for 8 hours or overnight.

2   Preheat barbecue to a high heat. Drain fillets and reserve marinade. Sear fillets on all sides, on lightly oiled barbecue. Move fillets to a cooler section of barbecue and cook, brushing frequently with marinade and turning several times, for 15 minutes or until cooked.

Oriental Pork Fillets, Barbecued Potato Skins

FELAFELS WITH MINTED YOGURT

Makes 15

- ☐ **200 g (7 oz) chickpeas, soaked overnight and drained**
- ☐ **90 g (3 oz) burghul (cracked wheat)**
- ☐ **2 cloves garlic, crushed**
- ☐ **$1/2$ cup/30 g/1 oz bread crumbs, made from stale bread**
- ☐ **1 egg, lightly beaten**
- ☐ **1 tablespoon lemon juice**
- ☐ **2 tablespoons chopped fresh coriander**
- ☐ **$1/2$ teaspoon garam masala**
- ☐ **$1/4$ teaspoon ground turmeric**
- ☐ **1 small red chilli, finely chopped**
- ☐ **freshly ground black pepper**
- ☐ **vegetable oil**
- ☐ **15 skewers, lightly oiled**

MINTED YOGURT
- ☐ **250 g (8 oz) natural yogurt**
- ☐ **1 tablespoon snipped fresh chives**
- ☐ **2 tablespoons finely chopped fresh mint**
- ☐ **freshly ground black pepper**

1   Place chickpeas in a large saucepan, cover with water and bring to the boil, then reduce heat and simmer for 35-40 minutes or until peas are cooked but still firm. Drain and set aside. Place burghul (cracked wheat) in a bowl, cover with $1/2$ cup/125 mL/4 fl oz water and set aside to soak for 15 minutes. Drain burghul and and press to remove any excess water.

2   Place chickpeas in a food processor or blender and process until smooth, add garlic, bread crumbs, egg, lemon juice, coriander, garam masala, turmeric and chilli and process until combined. Transfer to a bowl and mix in burghul. Season with black pepper. Chill for 1 hour.

3   Shape chickpea mixture into small oval-shaped patties. Chill for 30 minutes longer. Cook patties in hot oil for 4-5 minutes or until golden. Drain on absorbent kitchen paper, then thread onto skewers. Refrigerate until required. Preheat barbecue to a medium heat. Reheat felafels on lightly oiled barbecue for 4-5 minutes or until heated through.

4   To make Minted Yogurt, place yogurt, chives and mint in a bowl and mix to combine. Season to taste with black pepper. Serve with felafels.

Plants Balmain Garden Centre Plates Villa Italiana Basket Mondo Cane Tiles Fred Pazotti

Serving suggestion: Serve the felafels with shredded lettuce, chopped tomatoes, chopped parsley and chopped onions in warm pitta bread. To warm pitta bread, place on barbecue grill and cook for 30-45 seconds each side.

BARBECUED POTATO SKINS

Serves 4
Oven temperature 200°C, 400°F, Gas 6

- ☐ **6 large potatoes, scrubbed**
- ☐ **olive oil**

1   Bake potatoes in the oven for 1 hour or until tender. Remove from oven and set aside until cool enough to handle. Cut potatoes in half and scoop out flesh leaving a 5 mm/$1/4$ in thick shell. Reserve potato flesh for another use. Cut potato skins into large pieces and brush with oil.

2   Preheat barbecue to a medium heat. Cook potato skins on lightly oiled barbecue grill for 5-8 minutes each side or until crisp and golden.

Serving suggestion: Potato skins are delicious served with a dip of your choice.

Cook's tip: The reserved potato flesh can be used to make a potato salad to serve at your barbecue. It could also be used to make a potato curry, as a topping on a cottage pie, or to make croquettes.

Felafels with Minted Yogurt, Honey and Sage Pork Chops

GRILLED CORN BREAD

Grilled corn bread complements any barbecued meat, or can be served as part of a vegetarian meal.

Serves 6
Oven temperature 180°C, 350°F, Gas 4

- [ ] 1 cup/170 g/5^1/$_2$ oz corn meal (polenta)
- [ ] ^{3}/$_4$ cup/90 g/3 oz self-raising flour, sifted
- [ ] ^{1}/$_2$ teaspoon sugar
- [ ] 30 g/1 oz butter, melted
- [ ] 1 cup/250 mL/8 fl oz milk
- [ ] 1 egg
- [ ] olive oil

CORIANDER PESTO
- [ ] 3 large bunches fresh coriander
- [ ] 2 cloves garlic, crushed
- [ ] 60 g/2 oz pine nuts
- [ ] ^{1}/$_2$ cup/125 mL/4 fl oz olive oil
- [ ] 60 g/2 oz grated Parmesan cheese

1 Place corn meal (polenta), flour and sugar in a bowl and set aside. Whisk together melted butter, milk and egg. Add to corn meal mixture and mix to combine.

2 Spoon batter into a greased 20 cm/8 in round cake tin and bake for 15-20 minutes or until bread is cooked when tested with a skewer. Allow to stand in tin for 5 minutes before turning onto a wire rack to cool.

3 To make pesto, place coriander leaves, garlic and pine nuts in a food processor or blender and process to finely chop. With machine running, slowly pour in oil and process until smooth. Add cheese and process to combine

4 Preheat barbecue to a medium heat. Cut bread into wedges, brush lightly with oil and cook on barbecue for 2-3 minutes each side or until warm and golden. Top each wedge of bread with a spoonful of pesto and serve immediately.

PORK STEAKS WITH APPLE STUFFING

Serves 6

- [ ] 6 pork butterfly steaks

APPLE STUFFING
- [ ] 30 g/1 oz butter
- [ ] 1 onion, finely chopped
- [ ] 2 rashers bacon, finely chopped
- [ ] 1 apple, cored and finely chopped
- [ ] 1^1/$_2$ cups/90 g/3 oz bread crumbs, made from stale bread
- [ ] 1 egg, lightly beaten
- [ ] 155 g/5 oz mozzarella cheese, cut into small cubes
- [ ] 2 tablespoons chopped fresh parsley
- [ ] freshly ground black pepper

1 Place butterfly steaks on a board and, using a meat mallet, flatten slightly.

2 To make stuffing, melt butter in a frying pan and cook onion and bacon for 4-5 minutes or until bacon is crisp. Add apple and cook until apple is soft. Place apple mixture in a bowl, add bread crumbs, egg, mozzarella cheese and parsley and mix to combine. Season to taste with black pepper.

3 Preheat barbecue to a medium heat. Place spoonfuls of stuffing on one side of each butterfly steak, then fold over and secure with toothpicks. Cook on lightly oiled barbecue for 5-6 minutes each side or until steaks are cooked.

Above: Pork Steaks with Apple Stuffing
Right: Lamb Cutlets with Honey Butter, Grilled Corn Bread

LAMB CUTLETS WITH HONEY BUTTER

Serves 4

- [ ] **1 tablespoon vegetable oil**
- [ ] **1 clove garlic, crushed**
- [ ] **8 lamb cutlets**

HONEY BUTTER
- [ ] **90 g/3 oz butter, softened**
- [ ] **2 tablespoons chopped fresh mint**
- [ ] **1 tablespoon honey**
- [ ] **freshly ground black pepper**

1   To make Honey Butter, place butter, mint, honey and black pepper to taste in a small bowl and mix to combine. Place mixture on plastic food wrap and roll into a cylindrical shape. Refrigerate until hard.

2   Preheat barbecue to a medium heat. Place oil and garlic in a small bowl and mix to combine. Wrap ends of cutlet bones in aluminium foil to prevent burning during cooking. Brush cutlets with oil mixture and cook on barbecue plate (griddle) for 3 minutes each side or until lamb is tender.

3   Cut butter into small rounds and serve with cutlets.

Cook's tip: Interesting butter shapes can be made by using small biscuit cutter shapes.

Plants Balmain Garden Centre

Plants Balmain Garden Centre

Barbecue Secrets

No barbecue book would
be complete without a section on the
extras that seem to make everyone else's
barbecue a raging success. In this
chapter you will find many secrets
for perfect barbecuing.

Savoury Butters

Savoury butters are a great way to add taste after cooking – place a piece on a steak or in a baked potato. Garlic butter is probably the best known, but you can make a variety of tasty butters.

To make a parsley butter, place 125 g/4 oz softened butter, a dash of lemon juice, 1 tablespoon finely chopped fresh parsley and pepper to taste in a food processor or blender and process to combine. Shape butter into a log, wrap in plastic food wrap and refrigerate until firm.

This is the basic recipe for a savoury butter and the parsley can be replaced with any flavouring of your choice. Any fresh herbs can be used in place of the parsley – you might like to try chives, rosemary, thyme or basil. Combining different herbs can create an interesting flavour.

Other delicious flavours are horseradish, anchovy, roasted red or green pepper, curry paste, mustard, onion, spring onions, capers, finely grated lemon or lime rind.

BARBECUE SAUCE

Makes 1 cup/250 mL/8 fl oz

- ☐ 1 tablespoon vegetable oil
- ☐ 1 onion, chopped
- ☐ 1 clove garlic, crushed
- ☐ 1 teaspoon mustard powder
- ☐ 1 tablespoon Worcestershire sauce
- ☐ 1 tablespoon brown sugar
- ☐ 3 tablespoons tomato sauce
- ☐ 1 teaspoon chilli sauce
- ☐ 3/4 cup/185 mL/6 fl oz beef stock
- ☐ freshly ground black pepper

Heat oil in a saucepan and cook onion and garlic for 3-4 minutes or until soft. Stir in mustard powder, Worcestershire sauce, sugar, tomato sauce, chilli sauce and stock. Bring to the boil, then reduce heat and simmer for 8-10 minutes or until sauce reduces and thickens slightly. Season to taste with black pepper.

MEXICAN CHILLI SAUCE

Wonderful with steak, chops or sausages, this sauce will spice up any meal.

Makes 2 cups/500 mL/16 fl oz

- ☐ 2 tablespoons vegetable oil
- ☐ 2 small fresh red chillies, seeded and finely chopped
- ☐ 3 small fresh green chillies, seeded and finely chopped
- ☐ 3 cloves garlic, crushed
- ☐ 2 onions, finely chopped
- ☐ 1 tablespoon finely chopped fresh coriander
- ☐ 440 g/14 oz canned tomatoes, undrained and mashed
- ☐ 1 teaspoon brown sugar
- ☐ 1/2 teaspoon ground cinnamon
- ☐ 1/4 teaspoon ground cloves
- ☐ 1/4 teaspoon ground ginger
- ☐ 2 tablespoons lemon juice
- ☐ 3 tablespoons water

Heat oil in a frying pan and cook red and green chillies, garlic, onions and coriander for 2-3 minutes. Stir in tomatoes, sugar, cinnamon, cloves, ginger, lemon juice and water. Bring to the boil, then reduce heat and simmer for 15-20 minutes or until sauce reduces and thickens.

SWEET AND SOUR BARBECUE SAUCE

A sweet and sour sauce is always a popular accompaniment for chicken and pork, but is also delicious served with sausages and fish.

Makes 2 cups/500 mL/16 fl oz

- ☐ 1 tablespoon vegetable oil
- ☐ 1 small onion, chopped
- ☐ 1 red pepper, chopped
- ☐ 1 tablespoon soy sauce
- ☐ 2 tablespoons honey
- ☐ 1 tablespoon tomato paste (purée)
- ☐ 2 tablespoons cornflour
- ☐ 1/2 cup/125 mL/4 fl oz cider vinegar
- ☐ 1/2 cup/125 mL/4 fl oz chicken stock or water
- ☐ 440 g/14 oz canned pineapple pieces, drained

1 Heat oil in a saucepan and cook onion and red pepper for 4-5 minutes or until soft. Place soy sauce, honey, tomato paste (purée), cornflour and vinegar in a bowl and mix to combine.

2 Stir cornflour mixture into vegetables, then stir in stock or water. Cook, stirring, over a medium heat for 2-3 minutes or until sauce boils and thickens. Stir in pineapple pieces and cook for 2-3 minutes longer.

APPLE AND HORSERADISH SAUCE

Delicious served with beef and sausages, this condiment also makes an interesting accompaniment for barbecued fish.

Makes 1 cup/250 mL/8 fl oz

- ☐ 1/2 cup/125 mL/4 fl oz cream (double)
- ☐ 1 green apple, cored and grated
- ☐ 3 tablespoons horseradish relish
- ☐ freshly ground black pepper

Place cream in a bowl and whip until soft peaks form. Fold in apple and horseradish relish and season to taste with black pepper.

Barbecue Sauce, Mexican Chilli Sauce, Sweet and Sour Barbecue Sauce, Apple and Horseradish Sauce

70

WHAT'S IN A MARINADE?

A marinade tenderises the tough, moistens the dry and flavours the bland. It can be that secret ingredient that turns an otherwise ordinary piece of meat, fish, poultry or game into a taste sensation.

A marinade consists of an acid ingredient, an oil and flavourings – each ingredient playing an important role in the marinating process.

The acid ingredient: This can be lemon or lime juice, vinegar, wine, soy sauce, yogurt or tomatoes. The acid in a marinade tenderises foods such as beef, lamb, pork, poultry and seafood.

The oil: The moisturiser in the marinade. Olive and vegetable oils are the most popular but nut, herb or seed oils can also add an interesting flavour. A rule of thumb is that a marinade for barbecuing or grilling should contain at least 25 per cent oil, so each 1 cup/250 mL/8 fl oz of marinade, should include $^1/4$ cup/60 mL/2 fl oz oil.

The flavourings: Most commonly these are fresh or dried herbs and spices, garlic, ginger or onions.

How to marinate: As marinades contain acid ingredients, the food and marinade should be placed in stainless steel, enamel, glass or ceramic dishes. The marinade should come up around the sides of the food, but need not completely cover it. Turn the food several times during marinating. Food can also be marinated in a plastic food bag. This is particularly good for marinating large pieces of meat such as roasts. Place the food and marinade in the bag, squeeze out as much air as possible and seal with a rubber band or tie with a piece of string. Turn the bag several times during marinating.

How long to marinate: Marinating times can be anywhere between 15 minutes and 2 days. As a general rule, the longer you marinate the more tender and flavoursome the food will be. Food marinates faster at room temperature than in the refrigerator. But remember, in hot weather it is usually better to allow a longer marinating time in the refrigerator to ensure that the food stays safe to eat. Fish and seafood should not be marinated for longer than 30 minutes, as the acid ingredient in the marinade will 'cook' the fish. If marinating in the refrigerator, allow the food to stand at room temperature for 30 minutes before cooking to ensure even cooking of the marinated food.

Cooking marinated food: Drain the food well before cooking, especially when cooking in a frying pan or on a barbecue plate (griddle). Wet food will stew rather than brown. The remaining marinade can be brushed over the food several times during cooking.

COFFEE HONEY MARINADE

This delicious no-salt-added marinade is excellent for beef and lamb.

- ☐ **1 tablespoon honey**
- ☐ **1 tablespoon instant coffee powder**
- ☐ **$^1/4$ cup/60 mL/2 fl oz lemon juice**
- ☐ **2 cloves garlic, crushed**

1   Place honey, coffee powder, lemon juice and garlic in a small bowl and mix to combine.

2   Pour marinade over meat, cover and set aside to marinate.

WHITE WINE AND HERB MARINADE

This tasty marinade is ideal for fish and poultry. Choose the herbs that you like or that are in season.

- ☐ ³/₄ cup/185 mL/6 fl oz white wine
- ☐ ¹/₄ cup/60 mL/2 fl oz olive oil
- ☐ 2 spring onions, finely chopped
- ☐ 1 tablespoon chopped fresh herbs, or 1 teaspoon dried herbs

1 Place wine, oil, spring onions and herbs in a bowl and mix to combine.

2 Pour marinade over poultry or fish, cover and set aside to marinate.

RED WINE MARINADE

An excellent marinade for any type of red meat or game. For lighter meat, such as lamb, choose a lighter red wine – for example a Pinot Noir – while for game you can use a heavier red wine such as a Hermitage.

- ☐ 1¹/₂ cups/375 mL/12 fl oz red wine
- ☐ ¹/₂ cup/125 mL/4 fl oz olive oil
- ☐ 1 small onion, diced
- ☐ 1 bay leaf, torn into pieces
- ☐ 1 teaspoon black peppercorns, cracked
- ☐ 1 clove garlic, crushed
- ☐ 3 teaspoons finely chopped fresh thyme or 1 teaspoon dried thyme

1 Place wine, oil, onion, bay leaf, peppercorns, garlic and thyme in a small bowl and mix to combine.

2 Pour marinade over meat, cover and set aside to marinate.

LEMON HERB MARINADE

- ☐ ¹/₂ cup/125 mL/4 fl oz olive oil
- ☐ ¹/₄ cup/60 mL/2 fl oz lemon juice
- ☐ ¹/₄ cup/60 mL/2 fl oz white wine vinegar
- ☐ 1 clove garlic, crushed
- ☐ 1 teaspoon finely grated lemon rind
- ☐ 2 teaspoons finely chopped fresh parsley
- ☐ 2 teaspoons snipped fresh chives
- ☐ 3 teaspoons finely chopped fresh rosemary or 1 teaspoon finely chopped dried rosemary

1 Place oil, lemon juice, vinegar, garlic, lemon rind, parsley, chives and rosemary in a small bowl and mix to combine.

2 Pour marinade over meat or poultry, cover and set aside to marinate.

HOT CHILLI MARINADE

- ☐ ¹/₄ cup/60 mL/2 fl oz soy sauce
- ☐ ¹/₄ cup/60 mL/2 fl oz hoisin sauce
- ☐ ¹/₂ cup/125 mL/4 fl oz dry sherry
- ☐ 1 clove garlic, crushed
- ☐ 1 teaspoon grated fresh ginger
- ☐ 2 spring onions, finely chopped
- ☐ 1 teaspoon hot chilli sauce

1 Place soy sauce, hoisin sauce, sherry, garlic, ginger, spring onions and chilli sauce in a small bowl and mix to combine.

2 Pour marinade over meat or poultry, cover and set aside to marinate. Use the marinade as a baste when barbecuing.

Marinades add flavour and interest to meat, fish and poultry

At-a-Glance
Herb and Spice Guide
SAVOUR THE FLAVOUR WITH HERBS AND SPICES

HERB OR SPICE	MAIN DISHES	VEGETABLE DISHES	OTHER USES
Aniseed	seafood, pork and poultry dishes	salads, carrots and zucchini (courgettes)	cheese dips
Basil	fish dishes	tomato and green salads, baked vegetable dishes	dips, savouries, pasta sauces, stuffings, dressings, garnish
Bay	meat, fish and poultry dishes	vegetable casseroles	flavour pâtés and terrines
Cardamom	curries, spicy dishes of Indian and Middle Eastern origin	vegetable curries	pickles, savoury and sweet rice dishes
Cayenne Pepper	curries and spicy dishes		salad dressings, marinades
Chilli – fresh	all curries and spicy meat, poultry and fish dishes	spicy vegetables dishes	salad dressings, marinades, sauces, garnish
Chilli – powder	as for fresh chilli	spicy vegetable dishes	salad dressings, dips, pickles, sauces
Chives	all meat, chicken and fish dishes	salads, potato dishes	dips, herb butters, garnish
Coriander – fresh	Oriental and Middle Eastern cooking, seafood, poultry, meat dishes	green salads, oriental dishes	dips, pickles, garnish
Coriander – seed	curries and spicy meat, poultry, fish dishes	spicy vegetable dishes	yogurt dips, salad dressings
Cumin – seed	meat, poultry and fish dishes	cabbage, carrot and legume dishes	pickles, chutneys, marinades, rice dishes
Dill – fresh	fish, lamb and pork dishes	especially good with cucumber and cauliflower	fish sauces, cheese dips, garnish

HERB OR SPICE	MAIN DISHES	VEGETABLE DISHES	OTHER USES
Dill – seed	lamb, pork and fish dishes	cucumber, marrow, cabbage and carrots	pickles
Fennel – seed	chicken and fish dishes	potatoes	salad dressings, sauces for fish
Ginger – fresh	curries	vegetables curries	marinades
Ginger – ground	baked ham and fish dishes	vegetables curries and spicy legume dishes	pickles, spiced dishes such as mulled wine
Marjoram	all meat dishes	tomato dishes, potato and vegetable casseroles	sauces, herb butters, stuffings, marinades
Mint	lamb dishes, trout	new potatoes, peas, carrots, salads	summer drinks, mint sauce, stuffings, garnish
Mustard – powder	grilled meats	braised celery and leeks	salad dressings, stuffings, sauces
Mustard – seed	pork, rabbit, veal, some fish dishes	cabbage and celery	stuffings
Nutmeg	fish and chicken dishes	cabbage, carrots and root vegetables	pâtés
Oregano	Italian dishes, pasta and egg dishes, quiches, pizza, all meat dishes	onions, potatoes, peppers	pâtés, stuffings, marinades
Paprika	pork, beef, veal and fish dishes	legume dishes	rice dishes
Parsley	all fish, poultry and meat dishes, pasta	all vegetables and salads	dressings, stuffings, herb butters, garnish
Rosemary	lamb, fish and chicken dishes	eggplant (aubergines), tomatoes, cabbage	dressing, stuffings, pâtés, marinades
Saffron	chicken, fish and turkey dishes		savoury rice dishes
Sage	pork dishes	salads, vegetarian casseroles	stuffings
Tarragon	fish and chicken dishes	mushrooms, carrots, salads	sauces, stuffings, dressings, herb butters
Thyme	chicken and all meat dishes	most vegetable dishes	sauces, stuffings
Turmeric	curries, fish dishes		rice dishes

WHICH BARBECUE?

There are many different barbecues available. The one you choose will depend on your budget, how many people you regularly feed and whether barbecuing is usually a planned or an impromptu affair.

Gas barbecues: These barbecues contain lava rocks which are heated by gas burners. The lava rocks evenly distribute the heat and if you have a barbecue with multiple burners it is possible to have the rocks hot on one side and a medium heat on the other. The rack on which you cook the food is set above the rocks. Gas barbecues also require a gas bottle, which needs to be refilled on a regular basis – this is relatively inexpensive. When lighting a gas barbecue it is important to follow the manufacturer's instructions. If the barbecue does not ignite immediately, turn it off, wait for any build up of gas to disperse, then try again.

Wood or coal barbecues: The key to using these types of barbecues is patience and planning. These barbecues take up to an hour to heat, so you need to remember to light the barbecue well in advance.

Electric barbecues: These are ideal for people who want to barbecue indoors and, like gas barbecues, they produce almost instant heat.

HOW HOT?

The recipes in this book were cooked on a gas barbecue. Gas barbecues heat up very quickly and the heat is relatively easy to control, however if your barbecue uses coal, wood or barbecue fuel, you need to allow 30-45 minutes for coals to heat and 45 minutes to 1 hour for wood. The following is a guide for assessing the heat of these barbecues.

Hot fire: There will be a red glow showing through the thin layer of white ash and when you hold your hand 15 cm/6 in above the coals you will only be able to leave it there for 3 seconds. This fire is ideal for searing and quick cooking.

Medium fire: The red glow will be almost gone and the ash thicker and more grey in colour. When you hold your hand 15 cm/6 in above the coals you will be able to leave it there for 5-7 seconds. Most barbecuing is done on this heat.

Low fire: The red glow will have disappeared and there will be a thick coating of grey ash. This heat is ideal for slow cooking of foods.

The amount of heat reaching the food on these barbecues can also be controlled by moving the rack closer to or further away from the fire. If you have a wood barbecue, interesting flavours can be imparted to the food by using different types of wood. It is well to be aware that there are some plants that are poisonous and wood from those plants or chemically treated timber, is not suitable for barbecuing. Depending on where you live some of the following may be available: fruit woods, such as cherry and apple, which give a mild sweet flavour that is delicious when cooking pork, poultry and fish; grapevine cuttings – these give a delicate sweet flavour that is excellent for fish and poultry. Herbs such as rosemary and thyme also give interesting flavours when burned on the barbecue.

Equipment Check

Use this checklist to ensure that you have the basic equipment for successful barbecuing.

☐ oven mitt or cloth – important for handling hot skewers, racks and frying pans.

☐ tongs – these should be long-handled so that you can turn food without burning your hands. Use tongs for turning food, testing to see if steak is done (see page 53) and moving coals and hot racks.

☐ basting brushes – these are used to brush food with marinades, oil, butter or sauce during cooking.

☐ spatulas – essential for turning delicate foods, such as fish, so that they do not fall apart. The best type has a long, wide blade and a long handle.

☐ selection of sharp knives – use for preparation and carving cooked food.

☐ hinged grills, wire baskets – these come in many shapes and sizes for cooking whole fish and other foods that are difficult to turn. Always oil the grill or basket before using so that the food does not stick.

☐ skewers – bamboo or wooden skewers are good for quick cooking of foods. Before use, soak them in water to prevent them from burning during cooking. Before threading food onto bamboo or wooden skewers, lightly oil them so that the cooked food will slip off easily. Metal skewers are better for heavier foods.

☐ marinating pans and bowls – remember that most marinades contain an acid ingredient so the best choice of dish for marinating is glass, ceramic, stainless steel or enamel. Deep-sided disposable aluminium dishes are also good for marinating.

PLAY IT SAFE

As with any type of cooking, basic safety rules should always be observed. However with barbecuing there are a few extra that you need to remember.

✧ If you have a gas barbecue, before lighting it check that all the gas fittings and hose connections are tight.

✧ If your gas barbecue does not light first time, turn it off, wait 20 seconds and try again. This will ensure that there is no gas build-up.

✧ Always turn a gas barbecue off at the gas bottle as well as at the controls.

✧ Check the barbecue area before lighting the barbecue. Do not have the barbecue too close to the house and sweep up any dry leaves or anything that might catch fire if hit by a spark.

✧ Watch a lighted barbecue at all times. Keep children and pets away from hot barbecues and equipment.

✧ Do not barbecue in enclosed areas. If wet weather has forced you to move your barbecue undercover, ensure there is plenty of ventilation.

✧ Remember always to check the manufacturer's safety instructions that come with your barbecue.

Index